ELENA GOUDELIAS

After the Music

To Christina, who understands me like only a sister can.

Chapter 1

My last happy memory of Oak Plains was also one of my saddest. I'd been pulling out of the driveway of what used to be my childhood home when my gaze drifted upward and landed on the sunset. A sunset I'd seen countless times in the past. But this time, with the remnants of my old house reduced to nothing but a pile of ashes, the sky took center stage in its vastness. If it were any other day, I would have paused to marvel at the blanket of lavender and pink that stretched out above me. But it wasn't any other day. It was the day I'd lost a part of who I was, a part that I would never be the same without.

I shook my head to dispel the memory. With a sigh, I pressed my foot down on the gas, determined to get out of this town just as quickly as I'd entered it. *Just a quick pit stop*, I reminded myself. *That's all this is.*

As I turned onto Finch Lane, I raised the volume on the demo one of my clients had sent in. A mousy, hopeful budding artist by the name of Madison Brenner, she described her sound as a country/pop rock hybrid. To my trained ear, it sounded like Miranda Lambert and Kelly Clarkson had run into each other at the studio. I had to give Madison credit for melding the two genres together so seamlessly. My colleagues at Mountain Lion Records would envy me for tracking her down first.

I rolled up to a red light just as the crunch of electric guitars faded into the background. I made a mental note to let my boss know about the song. Lauren had spent the past several months lamenting the death of "real" music. "If I hear one more piece of auto-tuned garbage, I'm resigning," she'd announced as she passed by my desk one morning. "Does anyone even know how to play an instrument anymore?"

If nothing else, Lauren would appreciate Madison's demo for the way it showcased her guitar skills. The girl had talent, even if I sensed a note of hesitancy in her voice, as if she were awaiting formal permission to spread her wings and soar. But my boss didn't need to worry. I would find a way to coax her true voice out of her, just like I'd done with countless other clients who needed that extra push. After all, Lauren hadn't appointed me as Mountain Lion's resident A&R coordinator for nothing.

As the light turned green, unease clawed at my stomach. The road was beginning to look too familiar, the landscape an exact replica of the one etched into my memory. The girl I'd left behind on these dusty roads had lived a full life. A life punctuated by days spent strumming her guitar on the porch, drinking in the summer sunshine like the farm stand's fresh lemonade so sour it made her face pucker. A life where each day was a winding road that meandered every which way, leading wherever her grass-stained sneakers ended up.

As I reached the last house on Acorn Lane, I could almost hear the echoes of music and laughter that would ricochet off the emerald lawn all summer long. The silence that had harshly taken its place weighed down on my ears now, making the entire street feel like a ghost town.

I shut off the engine and opened the door, reminding myself that those days were long gone. Part of me wished my sister didn't live just down the street from my childhood home, where the memories were never further away than my own shadow.

I hopped out of the car and crossed the manicured lawn of my older sister's house. I'd barely approached the front door when the sweet, rich scent of Cassidy's famous cornbread wafted out. Even though our grandmother had been gone for ten of my twenty-eight years, that smell still reminded me of staying over at her house, where she'd spoiled us and dutifully stuffed us with her rich food until we could hardly move.

After sucking in a deep breath, I rang the bell and stood back, as if the door would combust at any moment. The dull thump of footsteps filtered through the screen door and came to an abrupt halt. As the door opened, Cassidy stood in the threshold, her curious eyes openly taking in the sight of me. "Bailey?"

I smiled, hoping that would make the stranger she saw evaporate into thin air. But the expression felt forced, unnatural, as if I'd hastily drawn the smile onto my face.

"Yup. It's me." I leaned in to give her a hug. "It's so nice to see you, Cass."

She smiled as we broke away, but her expression didn't dissolve the confusion in her eyes. I didn't blame her. Ever since I left my hometown six years ago at twenty-two, I'd only paid visits for birthdays and holidays. Of which today was

3

neither.

I forced a smile. "I was just a few towns away in Lenville for a press event, so I thought I'd stop by. I know you always make cornbread on Saturdays, and I just had to pick some up for my coworkers. I couldn't help but brag about how well you make it. Now the entire office wants to get their hands on it."

Cassidy's gaze traveled back to the kitchen, and understanding dawned on her barely a second later. "Oh, right. That's why you're here. I'll bring that right over."

I tried to ignore the disappointment that welled up inside me. I'd become the type of person who only stopped by when she needed something. How had everything gone so wrong over the past six years? It felt like just yesterday when I could talk freely to my sister about anything and expect nothing but understanding in return.

Cassidy returned, holding a Tupperware container of the fragrant dessert. I accepted it as she said, "I'm glad Grandma's recipe is living on. No one made cornbread like her."

"Well, yours comes pretty close," I said with a weak smile. I hated how stilted our conversation was, like we were reciting lines from an invisible script. I wanted to shake her and say, "It's me, Bailey! Don't you remember?"

But I was the only one to blame for my sister's stiffness, for the polite smile she normally reserved for strangers. I was the one who'd left when everyone needed me. I'd abandoned these dusty roads when they were calling out to me, begging me to give Oak Plains another chance.

Cassidy studied me for a moment. In a soft voice, she said, "You know you're always welcome here, Bailey."

Before I could respond, a girl with a head of unruly auburn curls came bobbing around the corner. "Hi, Aunt Bailey!"

Chapter 1

My face softened at the sight of Cassidy's six-year-old daughter, Leah. "Hey there, munchkin." As she wrapped her chubby arms around my legs, I smoothed down her wild curls. She was sporting a lemon-yellow dress that accentuated her sun-kissed skin.

Leah's eyes were wide as she looked up at me. "Are you coming to the summer concert?"

My face fell. I looked pointedly at the wall calendar that hung beside the door, feigning surprise. "Well, would you look at that. It's late June already. Guess this summer just crept up on me, huh?"

Leah planted a hand on each hip. "You still didn't say if you're coming."

In spite of myself, I had to smile. "I'll think about it, sweetie." I leaned down to kiss the top of her head. "I have a lot going on at work right now, but I'd love to come."

Cassidy looked at me steadily for a moment. She tenderly placed a hand on Leah's shoulder. "Why don't you go out to the backyard? Dad needs help with the garden."

The mention of the garden seemed to be an adequate distraction from the concert. She obediently scurried toward the back of the house, letting the patio door swing shut behind her.

"Eric doesn't need help with the garden, does he?"

Cassidy let out an exasperated sigh that was the only answer I needed. "Leah is right, Bailey. You can't skip the concert again this year."

"The show has been going on without me for years. Why does everyone need me there all of a sudden?"

My sister pursed her lips, her eyes drifting to the floor. "Annabelle was in an accident last month. She didn't make it."

A sharp pain seized my chest. I held on to the doorframe to steady myself. "Annabelle? As in Annabelle from church choir?"

Cassidy's nod was barely perceptible. "That's the one."

Annabelle had performed at the summer concert since I was in diapers. She never failed to captivate the crowd with her hypnotic guitar playing and voice that seemed to have drifted down from the heavens. I always felt ashamed to follow her performance with my pitiful guitar plucking.

"We need you, Bailey. You're the only one who knows how to keep the crowd as happy as she did. If you don't perform, we'll have to cancel the entire concert."

I blinked back tears, both for the distant friend I'd lost and for the past that was unraveling faster than I could stop it. I bit down on my lip, just barely managing to meet Cassidy's eyes. "The last time I sang in front of a crowd was…"

"I know." She rested her hand on my shoulder as her eyes reflected back the memories I'd worked so hard to bury. "We all remember."

I turned back toward the lawn. "I… I'll have to think about it."

"Please, Bailey. This town never stopped caring about you. It's time you started giving back to them."

I gripped the Tupperware tightly, as if it were the last shard of confidence I had left. "Thanks for the cornbread, Cassidy. I'll call you."

With a tight smile, I turned to my car and slid into the driver's seat. I released a long breath and turned on the stereo. As the next demo started to play, I backed out of the driveway without turning my eyes to the house. My mother's words drifted toward me then, as if the wind were carrying them through the open window of the car. *Always tuning out the world with music, Bailey. When are you going to take off those headphones and step out into the world?*

I raised the volume in response, as if I were still the sullen thirteen-year-old girl she'd said those words to. Back then, my playlist had been bruised with the melancholy shades of Norah Jones and the rough edges of Nirvana. I'd sworn it was only a phase, yet I found myself sinking back into that dark world after the fire. It was as if I'd never truly left it. As if I were simply waiting for the next time it would suck me back in.

I rolled down the window while the next future country superstar, a Texas native named Jake, plucked away at a banjo and filled the car with his syrupy-sweet voice. He would surely be a hit with the ladies. His crooning melody reminded me that I'd come a long way since that dark period six years ago, no matter how much my sister's worried eyes tried to convince me otherwise.

I merged onto the highway and began the three-hour journey west toward my home in suburban Pittsburgh. Oak Plains sat squarely in the middle of central Pennsylvania, which meant it took about an hour of driving before I reentered civilization. For so long, the bucolic setting that accompanied my country music had been a breath of fresh air. Now, it felt so lonely that I couldn't get out of the stifling town fast enough.

As I watched shopping malls swallow up vast stretches of verdant land, my phone vibrated next to me. Seeing Lauren's name on the screen, I furrowed my brow. My boss must have been in a dire emergency if she was calling me on a Saturday.

"Hi, Lauren." I fumbled for the speakerphone button. "Is everything all right?"

"Not unless you fix things. South Side just canceled their appearance at the Reverb Music Festival, and seeing as they were the main act, there's no point in covering the event anymore. I need you to find another musical event to attend. Pronto. I know you'll snatch up something good, since you seem to have a knack for tracking down the biggest events on the music scene."

"How big are you thinking?"

"Big enough to get people talking. Ideally, they should already be talking about it."

An idea was peeking into my mind, an idea that wasn't fully formed yet. It didn't even fulfill Lauren's requirements, and I was pretty sure she would dismiss it without a second thought. But it was beginning to look like my only ticket out of the hole I'd dug myself into at my sister's house. A cunning smile crept onto my face. "How does a summer concert sound? My hometown puts on a big show in our local park every August. There'll be performances from all types of genres. Country, rock, pop. You name it. It'll be sure to cause a buzz."

There was a pause. "Didn't you say you came from a small town? I don't see how that would generate much of a buzz."

"Well, it might've been a small event in the past, but I can guarantee this year will be the biggest we've ever seen. People will still be talking about the set list I've put together months from now."

"You haven't let me down yet, so I'll take your word for it. But if this turns out to be a flop, we'll have to settle for that Nickelback knockoff band that Jeremy dug up from some sad corner of YouTube. Please don't make me resort to that."

"Don't worry. I've got it all under control."

I slipped my phone into my bag while my brilliant plan came into focus. Just because Cassidy wanted me to stick around for the concert didn't mean I had to perform in it. Madison and

Chapter 1

Jake's demos had already proved to be brimming with promise, and aspiring musicians like them were hungry for any form of exposure. I would be doing them a favor by handing them this opportunity.

I reached for my phone again and called Cassidy without missing a beat. "Hey. About the concert—"

"I *knew* you would change your mind. Even after all these years, I still know how to talk you into things."

"Well, you're half right. I am coming to the show. But I won't be up on stage."

She hesitated. "What, are you going to sing from your seat or something?"

"I'm not singing at all. But someone else will."

"Really, Bailey. This isn't the time for jokes."

"I'm not joking. It's my job to look for new talent, so it shouldn't be hard to find the best artists for our town's concert. I'll have a whole lineup of musicians ready by the end of July, and we'll sign the most talented ones. No one will even remember that I was supposed to perform."

A weighted sigh leaked out of the speaker. "You go through so much trouble to get out of things you don't want to do. I don't know whether to be sad or amazed."

"I'm just trying to help."

We both knew that wasn't the real reason I couldn't face a crowd again, but she didn't comment on it. Instead, she said, "Well, as long as you'll be there, I guess that's all that matters." I heard the smile in her voice as her next words left her mouth. "It's good to have you back, Bailey."

Only then did I realize I'd left the door wide open, letting the past stroll right through it.

Chapter 2

The sweet smell of lavender tickled my nostrils as I climbed Cassidy's front steps the following weekend. Somewhere inside that scent was a memory that I wasn't ready to unearth. Small, pesky reminders of the life I'd lived back then were woven into the fabric of my sister's house, echoing the past I couldn't leave at her doorstep.

As I walked through the door, my sister was coming down the stairs. She smiled. "I just finished getting your room ready. I'm so glad you decided to stay here, Bailey. So are Eric and the kids."

I smiled hesitantly. "Thanks, Cass. But I don't want you getting too used to me around here. My boss isn't thrilled about my remote-work setup." As an A&R coordinator, I spent the majority of my time outside the office, either attending shows or meeting artists in the recording studio. But Lauren liked to have her employees within arm's reach if she ever needed to sequester us in the office for any reason.

"I know. But that doesn't mean we won't still do everything we can to convince you to stay in Oak Plains."

I plopped my bag onto the kitchen counter. "Unless you find some way to erase that summer, there's no chance of that happening."

I didn't meet her eyes as I rummaged through my bag. I knew there was no need for me to clarify which summer I was talking about. The aftershocks of that humid August evening still rolled through my body, holding me hostage in an ever-present state of grief. Cassidy saw it. Eric saw it. Everyone who came into contact with me seemed to see it as clearly as my wavy golden-brown hair.

Cassidy stepped out into the garden for a moment. She paused to study the bird feeder as if she were seeing it for the first time. When she returned to the kitchen, she let out a theatrical sigh. "We seem to be out of birdseed. I would run out and get more, but I have to drop off Leah at dance practice soon. Would you mind picking up some new seed at the hardware store?"

Normally, I would have inquired about her strange tone of voice, but I'd been rooting around for an excuse to get some air ever since I arrived. "Sure. Cooper Hardware, right?"

A mixture of relief and surprise crossed Cassidy's face, as if she'd been expecting me to drag my feet. "That's the one. Here, I'll show you the exact type I need."

After snapping a picture of the packet, I grabbed my bag and keys and headed to the store. Cooper Hardware sat on an out-of-the-way road, a good few miles from the other main shops in Oak Plains. I found a parking space—not a huge feat in a town like ours—and cut the engine. After retrieving my bag, I traipsed into the store and surveyed the space. I ducked under the Garden & Outdoor sign and scanned the shelves for the product Cassidy needed.

I picked up a packet of birdseed and squinted at it under the harsh fluorescent lights, trying to determine if it matched the photo I'd taken. I was vaguely aware of heavy footsteps coming up from behind me, but I was too focused on the task at hand to pay them any mind. I sighed, wishing I'd taken a clearer picture of the product before I left.

I'd just started to tap out a text to Cassidy when a male voice droned, "Need any help, ma'am?"

"Yes, actually." I pulled up the photo of Cassidy's birdseed. "I was looking for..."

My voice trailed off as I looked up at the man for the first time. Despite the baseball cap pulled down low over his eyes and the newly grown beard adorning his face, I recognized him immediately. Shock slowly registered on his face as he absorbed the sight of me. We stood there for a weighted moment, unmoving. I could have sworn neither of us was breathing.

"Well, I'll be damned," he said in his southern drawl. He planted his hands on his hips and regarded me closely. "Bailey Flynn, is that really you?"

I swallowed, trying to find my voice. "Dustin?"

"That's what they call me." In the eye of my memory, I was sitting in my junior-year geometry class again as Dustin Cooper told me he'd just moved here from Georgia. *Little town called Mapleville. Kinda like Oak Plains, plus the southern charm,* he'd said with a grin.

He crossed his arms as his lips twisted into a smirk. "This the same girl who swore she was never coming back to Oak

Plains?"

My face burned. In response, I showed him the packet of birdseed and held up my phone. "I'm not sure if these two match."

He smiled and shook his head. "Pretending the past doesn't exist, huh? You haven't changed at all, Bailey."

The sound of my name on his lips activated something inside me. Something that threw off the rhythm of my heart. I cleared my throat. "I just came here to run an errand. My sister expects me back soon."

He still hadn't wiped his amused grin off his face. "So, Cassidy sent you here?"

"Yes, that's my—" I stopped short as the most obvious thing in the world walloped me in the face. I knew Cassidy had been acting strangely, but her intentions hadn't dawned on me until now. "She didn't actually need birdseed, did she?"

Dustin just laughed, a hearty sound that rippled out of his husky frame. He had the kind of laugh that drew anyone to his presence, like a bumblebee to honeysuckle. I caught myself starting to smile and promptly wiped it off my face. This wasn't the time to joke around with the guy who used to sit next to me in math class. And it certainly wasn't the time to notice that his eyes were gleaming, just like they had every time he stole a glance at me in high school.

Desperate to take the spotlight off myself, I asked, "When did you start working here? Growing up, I remember your dad running the whole store."

"Couple years ago. My dad had to step back and take some time off. He's no spring chicken anymore, and this job has been tough on him." A smile graced his face again. "Of course, it makes it easier when I get to help beautiful women find birdseed."

My cheeks flamed as I put the item back on the shelf. "Well, I won't be needing this anyway. I'm going to have to give my sister a good talking-to."

I turned and headed for the door before I could humiliate myself any further. But I hadn't even made it to my car when I heard Dustin call my name.

I turned around and saw him approaching me. He removed his baseball cap and ran a hand through his brown hair, his eyes squinting in the late-morning sunlight. He leaned against my car and looked at me. "You don't always have to go running off, you know."

"I didn't run."

He took a step toward me, a frown deepening the lines on his forehead. "What happened, Bailey? What stole your smile?"

"You know the answer." My voice trembled despite all my efforts to steady it.

"That was six years ago," he said gently. "You can't live in the past forever."

I clutched my car key, ignoring the pain as it dug into my palm. "I have to go." But even as I said it, I couldn't bring myself to leave.

He studied me, his brown eyes heavy with sadness. "You're still afraid, aren't you?"

I was afraid. Afraid that I could never again be the person I was before that summer. Afraid that what happened had changed me irreversibly. But, most of all, I was afraid of giving myself permission to hope that the future would somehow be different. Because I knew better than that after everything I'd gone through.

"Those days are over," I said levelly. "Nothing will ever be the same as it was before that summer. And I'd really appreciate it if everyone would stop acting like I can just go back to the person I used to be."

With that, I unlocked the car and climbed inside. Just before I shut the door, Dustin said, "The person you used to be is still somewhere inside of you. I can see it, and so can everyone else. Otherwise, we wouldn't have waited all this time for you to give Oak Plains another chance."

His words rolled through my mind during the entire drive back to Cassidy's house. It wasn't until I reached her driveway that I realized he'd just admitted he'd been waiting six years to see me again.

* * *

When I walked through the front door without the birdseed, Cassidy had a smirk perched on her face that closely resembled Dustin's. "Got a little distracted, I see."

I set my bag down more forcefully than I intended. "If you wanted to set me up with Dustin, you should've just told me."

"Honey, we both know you wouldn't have gone if I'd told you."

I grabbed the suitcase I'd left in the foyer and dragged it toward the staircase. Cassidy sighed. "You do realize that Dustin's had a thing for you since junior year of high school, right? He still asks about you whenever I see him. And all this time, you've just closed yourself off from him. Even when he tried to talk to you in school, you never gave him the time of day."

"You know I wasn't ready for a boyfriend back then. Trying to survive high school is hard enough without the stress of a relationship. Besides, it wouldn't be fair to Dustin to start something with him if I wasn't serious about it."

"I know, and I don't blame you. I don't think either of you were ready, to be honest. Dustin had recently broken up with Gina, remember? Then college kept you two apart for four years. The timing wasn't right then, but it is now. I can already see how much you've changed. He's a great guy, Bailey, and he's worth it. You don't know what could happen if you gave him a chance."

"That's the problem. I don't know."

Cassidy hesitated, as if she were carefully weighing her next words. She met my eyes. "Not everything in life is a setup for disappointment, you know."

I tightened my grip on the suitcase handle. "Well, when I left the house the morning of the summer concert, I had no idea I would never see it again. So forgive me for being overly cautious."

I lugged my suitcase to the guest room and slammed the door behind me before sinking to the floor. As I buried my head in my hands, I replayed the conversation with Cassidy in my head, my face burning in shame as my combative tone echoed back to me. That hadn't been me at all. That had been an impostor who'd spoken through me, wounding the person she loved.

Dustin's words returned to me then: *The person you used to be is still somewhere inside of you.* I wanted to believe he was right with every fiber of my being. But I knew all the same that it was easier to keep that version of me buried along with the past. Because once I dragged her out again, she would only leave me disappointed.

I stared out at the street I'd lived on for most of my life, my mind drifting to a place I wasn't yet ready to visit. All these years, the worst night of my life had come back to me in bits and pieces, as if my brain were trying to protect me from the memory in its entirety. But now that I'd made the decision to stay in Oak Plains for a while, I knew keeping the past at arm's length was a waste of time.

I closed my eyes and saw myself up on stage that August evening. I was twenty-two at the last summer concert, which had been the biggest one our town had ever seen. Word had spread throughout Pennsylvania and rippled through the neighboring states, bringing spectators from Pittsburgh all the way to the Catskills. I'd never felt prouder to call myself an Oak Plains resident as I did that day.

Evelyn, my childhood best friend, had been my backup vocalist for the tenth year running. I always faced the crowd with more confidence when I had Evelyn by my side, the two of us hitting the same high notes we used to belt out of our makeshift hairbrush microphones in our childhood bedrooms. She was the one who had introduced me to country music when she'd gifted me a copy of Loretta Lynn's *Van Lear Rose* for my fifteenth birthday. As I lost myself in the spellbinding lyrics and soothing melodies, I'd discovered a unique kind of beauty in the rural landscape that I'd shunned for most of my youth.

Evelyn had just launched into her first guitar solo when I heard the sirens. They seemed distant at first, as if they belonged to a separate universe. Such a jarring sound was rare in our peaceful town, and it didn't take long for heads to start turning. My singing came to an abrupt halt. A moment later, Evelyn stopped strumming her guitar. After several minutes that seemed to stretch out indefinitely, I glimpsed Ruth from across the street rushing over to Cassidy, who had been watching me from the front row. Cassidy went completely still as Ruth spoke to her. When my sister finally lifted her eyes to mine, her face was as white as the shirt she was wearing.

Everything that happened next was a blur. Only certain details stood out against the hazy landscape of my memory, like the look of acute horror on Evelyn's face when Ruth told us what had happened and the way the summer heat suddenly felt oppressive. I had no recollection of putting down my guitar and leaving the stage. All I remembered was that I started running.

I ran past the park, past the church, past Evelyn's house, past every corner of the town that no longer belonged to me. I didn't stop running until I stumbled onto my front lawn and watched Ruth's words play out before my eyes like a twisted horror film. I wasn't looking at my house anymore. I was looking at white-hot flames devouring an empty shell that had once been my refuge. The rooms that used to hold so much love and joy were columns of smoke, the windows I used to gaze out of now unseeing, soulless eyes.

The firefighters later informed us that one of the stovetop burners had been left on. The leftover grease in one of the pans had caught fire, spreading faster than anyone could stop it. I didn't hear the rest of what they said. My mind was a rapid succession of images. The pan on the stovetop, the burner lit beneath it, me running up the stairs to grab my guitar for the show. I'd been helping my parents cook up a feast for the event, but I hadn't realized until that moment that I'd neglected to shut off the burner. Such a simple step, yet it ended up costing us our entire home.

As I stared at the skeleton that stood before our eyes, the weight of what I'd done was too much for me to bear. I collapsed onto the soft bed of grass, unable to do so much as lift my head. My body trembled as I rested my cheek on the cool blades, unable to shed a single tear. Crying would have been a relief. Instead, I lay there helplessly and took frantic, gasping breaths, as if there were a shortage of air around me.

I tucked my feet underneath me and opened my eyes, willing the present to blot out the past. But the passage of time had done little to abate the pain. The burden of guilt had followed me like an unwelcome shadow for the past six years. If I hadn't left the burner on, my family would still have a home. I'd been so wrapped up in my music and the exciting night that awaited me that I didn't realize I was about to change our lives irrevocably. Because it wasn't just the house we'd lost. It was the culmination of the dream my parents had of building their own home and starting a family in it, which they'd made a reality thirty years ago. It was all the artwork my mother had created herself and proudly displayed throughout the house, an imprint of who she was. It was the small leather-bound songbook that held every song I'd written since I was sixteen. And it was the home that was supposed to be passed down to Cassidy and me so we could fill it with our own memories one day.

I swore to myself that I would never make music again. I didn't deserve to. The longer I silenced my voice, the more it seemed like a just form of self-punishment. It didn't matter how many times my parents or sister reassured me that it was an accident, that the important thing was that no one had been hurt. I'd seen the pain in their eyes as the firefighters detailed the extent of our loss. And when my parents moved down to Florida a few months later to care for my widowed paternal grandmother, I knew they'd partly made their decision because they couldn't stand to be in Oak Plains anymore. To drive by an empty lawn and constantly be reminded of what they'd lost. It was, after all, the same reason I'd left town the morning after the fire.

I rose from the floor and stepped back out into the hall, needing a distraction. When I reached the foot of the stairs, I caught a glimpse of Jade, Cassidy's eldest daughter. Just the sight of one of my nieces made my heart feel lighter, and I found myself breathing a little easier than I had when I was all alone with my thoughts.

Jade was facing her mother with a hand pressed defiantly to her hip. Her blue eyes were rimmed with jet-black eyeliner, and her blond hair was streaked with bright purple. She had tiny white earbuds jammed into her ears and was tapping away at her phone while Cassidy tried to talk to her. As I studied Jade's sullen expression, something about her struck me. She reminded me of the thirteen-year-old girl I'd once been, choosing the world inside her headphones over the world that surrounded her.

"You need to stop staring at your phone, Jade. And what is that music you have on all the time? No wonder you're always so angry."

"Oh my *God*, Mom. Stop standing outside my room!"

"You had your speakers on full blast. I heard it all the way from downstairs."

"Why do you care so much about what I listen to?" Without waiting for an answer, she stomped up to her room in her chunky lace-up combat boots.

"Jade! You come back down right now and take those boots off!"

Knowing she was fighting a losing battle, Cassidy closed her eyes and sighed. "I don't know why I still try to reason with her."

"Sometimes I think I might want to have kids, but then I

remember they're going to be thirteen one day."

Cassidy managed a tired smile. "Couldn't have said it better myself."

"Look, I'm sorry for the way I talked to you before. I don't know what got into me. It's like being in this town is dredging up all the horrible memories from that summer."

"I know you didn't mean it. You still have hints of the old Bailey inside you, whether you want to believe it or not."

"That's what Dustin said to me before," I muttered.

She raised an eyebrow. "Well, you should listen to him. He's wise for his age."

Ignoring her, I opened the fridge and started idly scouring its contents.

"You know," Cassidy began, "Jade reminds me of you as a teenager in a lot of ways. Maybe you should try talking to her. Since she's given up on listening to me, it's worth a try."

I thought of Jade again, picturing her rebellious clothing and sour expression. Cassidy was right—she resembled me *too* closely. It was like stepping back into that period of my life and living through those dark days again.

I released my grip on the fridge handle and turned to face my sister. Her face was kind, patient. I knew she deserved to see more of me than the faint shadow I'd revealed to her so far.

I drew in a breath. "For so long, I thought I was destined to be like Jade for the rest of my life. Always trapped in my own head and wearing misery like it was some new fashion trend. Then I started making music when I was sixteen, and it scared me, Cass. I was scared of how happy it made me because I'd never felt like that before. I think a part of me was secretly waiting for something bad to happen to take all that joy away from me." I cast my eyes to the floor. "Then the fire happened, and I was back to being the miserable girl I'd always been. A part of me thinks that's who I truly am, and all those years I spent living my passion were just a fluke."

When I looked up at Cassidy again, her eyes were weighed down with so much sorrow that I had to look away. Now that my bare feelings were out in the open, they seemed stark. Naked. I had the sudden urge to march over to the bay window and close the blinds, as if they could protect all the other truths I'd guarded so carefully inside me.

"You know that's not true," she said quietly. "There's so much happiness out there waiting for you. But if you keep closing yourself off like this, you'll never find it." Her voice grew serious. "I was scared out of my mind when I had Jade at nineteen. I didn't know the first thing about being a mother. It was like someone had shoved an exam in front of me that I never got around to studying for. But Jade also let me experience more joy than I'd ever thought was possible. I don't want you to miss out on that just because you're so focused on the possibility of something going wrong."

The sound of booted footsteps shifted our attention to the staircase. Jade rolled her eyes as she made her way down. "Are you talking about when I was born again?" She stopped when she noticed me for the first time. Her brow furrowed. "What are you doing here?"

"Is that how you greet your aunt?" Cassidy snapped.

I smiled at Jade. "It's okay. You don't have to fake politeness around me."

"Thank goodness." She gave her mother a pointed look and rushed to the foot of the stairs. Just as she did, Cassidy said, "Shoes, please."

I pulled back at the sight of Jade's icy stare, then turned to see my sister's reaction. But her face was calm, unaffected, as if her daughter gave her the death glare on a daily basis.

After yanking off her combat boots and tossing them off to the side, Jade turned to Cassidy with wide, pleading eyes. "Alexis has tickets to the Electric Ashes concert next Friday. Can I please, please go? Everyone's gonna be there."

"Well, not everyone needs to work on their attitude. Why don't you try being a little nicer to your family first?"

"But Aunt Bailey said—"

"I don't care what she said. And you need to help out around the house more, young lady."

I knew this wasn't the time to encourage her, but I couldn't help myself. "The Electric Ashes? I thought only old ladies like me still listened to their music. I've always wanted to see them live."

I could see Cassidy glowering at me from the corner of my eye, but I pretended I didn't notice. Jade's eyes lit up as she looked at me, and it struck me how beautiful she was behind the heavy makeup and permanent grimace. "You should come with us, Aunt Bailey!" She turned to her mother with a satisfied expression. "See? Now I have an adult to supervise me. Problem solved."

"Not so fast. You're not ready to go until I say you are."

She groaned. "Aunt Bailey is so much cooler than you." Pushing past her mom, she stepped out onto the front porch and slammed the door behind her.

Cassidy gave me a sidelong glance. "For the record, if a thirteen-year-old thinks you're cool, you're doing something wrong."

I shrugged. "Hey, if I get an Electric Ashes show out of it, I'm fine with it."

"Don't you need to focus on finding someone to perform at our concert?"

"I already have a couple of candidates lined up. I listened to their demos on my way here yesterday, and they both have a lot of potential. I just need to track down a few more promising artists. But considering that's my day job, I'm not worried."

Cassidy looked past what I was saying, into a place deep in my eyes. In a quiet voice, she asked, "When was the last time you sang, Bailey?"

Her words found a weak spot inside me, a spot that was still tender to the touch. It had been my first week in Ackerdale, the suburb of Pittsburgh I'd moved to after running away from Oak Plains. Jackie, my next-door neighbor and the closest thing I had to a friend in the entire town, had stumbled upon the lyrics to a song I'd written long before the ill-fated summer concert. After she'd prodded me at length to sing it for her, I'd reluctantly obliged. It wasn't until I opened my mouth that I heard how passionless my melody was. It was as if the words were coming solely from my brain, not my heart. I couldn't help but feel like what happened that summer had robbed me of my love for music.

"About a week after the show," I said, my voice barely above a whisper.

"Oh, Bailey."

Maybe it was something in her voice, or the reality of the last six years finally sinking in. But as I stood there in the middle of the living room, a wave of nostalgia swept over me, the force of it so powerful I almost gasped for breath. I missed the innocent, carefree person I'd been all those years ago, blissfully unaware that such a beautiful thing could be taken away from her. I wanted to hold her close, to tell her to savor the life she had, because it wasn't meant to last forever.

Most of all, though, I wanted to warn her that the night of the concert would be the last time she would genuinely enjoy singing. Because everyone looked at things differently when they knew they were seeing them for the last time.

Chapter 3

That Friday night, the PA system pumped Top 40 hits through the packed concert arena as I looked for my seat. Everyone was here to see pop supergroup the Violet Hearts, but I'd come to the Stevenson Center in Harrisburg to see Madison Brenner. Madison, one of the artists whose demo I played on the way to Cassidy's house, was the opening act at tonight's show. This was my chance to see how comfortable she was in front of a crowd. Some artists were natural-born performers, while others seemed to realize mid-concert that they weren't singing in their bedrooms anymore. Those were always the most painful to watch.

I settled into my seat and let the energy of the arena sizzle through my veins. Most of the shows I attended for work were held in small venues where scattered applause replaced the passionate screams of larger crowds. Even though the show hadn't started yet, my heart was still thumping in anticipation of the moment the lights went down. I'd forgotten about how thrilling it was to be a part of something so big.

"Bailey?"

I almost didn't hear my name among the din of the audience. When I turned around to see who it was, I nearly dropped my water bottle.

"Evelyn?" I studied my friend, who looked like she'd been frozen in time over the past six years. Everything from her signature long braid to her cowboy boots was an exact replica of the girl who used to play guitar alongside me on stage.

Evelyn hopped down the two steps that separated us and wrapped me in a vanilla-scented hug. The way she made me feel right at home despite all the time that had separated us made tears prick my eyelashes. I wasn't the same Bailey anymore, but she had never stopped being Evelyn.

When we pulled away, her hazel eyes were bright. "I can't believe you're actually here. The last time I saw you, you were getting the whole reception hall to dance to Shania Twain at my brother's wedding."

I laughed. "Unfortunately, I remember that."

"I always catch glimpses of the old Bailey after you've had a few drinks." She smiled in a nostalgic kind of way, as if she were trying to find that version of me somewhere in my eyes.

I glanced around at the rows of seats that were quickly filling up. "So, you're into dance pop now? The last place I expected to run into you is a Violet Hearts concert."

She rolled her eyes. "I'm here with my ten-year-old cousin. Her mom had to work late, so she put me in charge of supervising her." She threw me a questioning look. "What about you? This is exactly the kind of music you used to make fun of when we were younger."

"Actually, I'm just here for the opening act. My boss needs me to find some artists to perform at the summer concert. Madison Brenner seems to have a lot of potential from what I've heard so far."

Evelyn studied me for a moment. "You're still not ready to go back onstage, are you?"

I swallowed. "Not exactly."

The loud conversation around us devoured the awkward silence that followed. As I dug around for a new topic of conversation, a chubby girl with light blond hair and freckles materialized at Evelyn's side, pulling on her arm. "Come *on*. The show's going to start soon."

"I'll be right there, Olivia." Evelyn turned around to face me. "I have to run back to my seat. But I'll catch up with you after the show, okay?"

As she followed her cousin back up the steps, I shifted my attention to the stage below where Madison's band had been setting up. Now, the drummer was tapping out a steady beat while Madison strummed a few opening chords on her acoustic guitar. I tuned out the residual chatter around me as I let the music envelop me. Even when the real world was messy, I could always find refuge in the alternate world that music allowed me to escape into. A much more beautiful, harmonious world that I often preferred over the one outside my window.

The song was in full swing now, and I recognized it as the tune I'd played on my way into Oak Plains. Madison started off strong, her voice projecting the first long note throughout the arena. I was close enough to observe her movements, to see how she kept her eyes closed in a dreamlike way while she sang. Her voice had a hushed quality, like she was singing a lullaby. It closely mimicked the way she sounded on the demo, and I couldn't help but worry that it stemmed from a lack of confidence rather than an artistic choice.

She wrapped up the first song and segued into the next one. Things appeared to be going well during the first verse, and I silently commended her for picking up confidence. But just as she was about to begin the second verse, I saw the panic on her face. Her eyes darted across the crowd, as if the audience knew the lyrics that she couldn't remember. I held my breath while I watched her, wordlessly cheering her on. I remembered forgetting the lyrics during an impromptu performance at a bar with Evelyn about ten years ago. My face probably hadn't looked too different from Madison's as my memory betrayed me. But Evelyn had been quick to supply me with the missing lyrics, and it was almost as if my slipup had never happened.

Of course, there was a world of a difference between a casual bar performance and an appearance at a headlining tour. That difference was evident on Madison's face as she struggled to salvage her performance. The poor girl looked like a deer in headlights, and the car was about to collide with her at any moment. A few spectators around me exchanged nervous glances and whispers while others had the audacity to point their phones toward Madison and record her humiliating moment.

Her bass guitarist finally stepped up to the mic and cleared his throat. "Uh, we're just going to take a quick break."

For a horrifying moment, I watched as Madison, head bowed, removed her guitar from her neck and started to head backstage. Just before she did, though, a single voice tore through the confused chatter scattered across the arena.

For a moment, it was quiet except for the distant but determined voice belting out the lyrics that had left Madison by the wayside. Slowly, Madison turned around and searched for the owner of the voice. When she caught sight of the girl who must have been in her early teens, relief washed over her visibly. She listened for a moment as the girl continued carrying her tune, then walked up to the edge of the catwalk where her devoted fan stood just below.

"What's your name?" Madison asked as she bent down toward the girl.

"Sarah," she said into the microphone, clearly starstruck.

"Looks like it's your lucky day, Sarah. Why don't you come on up here and help me out with this next song?"

Sarah, who looked like she'd just walked into a daydream, nodded vigorously. "I'd love to."

Madison had barely led Sarah toward her own microphone stand when Sarah seized the mic like she'd been planning on taking over the stage all along. Her voice complemented Madison's beautifully. As they sang together, Madison's voice became steadily more assertive, and she even started swinging her hips to the beat. I was glad to see her recovering so well, but I feared what would've happened if there hadn't been a fan in the audience who knew her songs better than she did.

The crowd roared at the conclusion of the performance, but I couldn't tell if they were cheering for Madison or Sarah. I clapped distractedly, unable to hide my disappointment. Offering Madison a spot on the summer concert set list was too big of a risk now. If she blanked out again, I would make a fool of myself in front of the entire town. Worse, I might lose my job.

I dispelled my worries by telling myself I would work on Madison. All she needed was a push in the right direction, which was exactly what Sarah had given her. She would be unstoppable once I helped her find her confidence.

A second opener followed Madison's performance, and the Violet Hearts launched into their set after arriving fashionably late. Even though their music wasn't to my taste, I had to admit they put on an entertaining show. I glanced behind me every now and then and caught a glimpse of Olivia, who looked like she was having the time of her life. It was like stepping into a time machine and watching myself at my very first concert, which had been Carrie Underwood's 2006 tour. Evelyn and I exchanged a knowing smile, and I had a feeling we had the same memory flashing through our minds.

As the band started to wrap up its last song, I grabbed my bag and slipped through the closest exit. The last thing I wanted was to be caught in a stampede of teenage girls on my way to the parking lot. Once I was safely outside the venue, I scanned the stream of fans that charged out of the building in search of Evelyn. I found my friend walking beside Olivia, who hadn't torn her eyes away from her phone since she stepped out of the arena.

I waved Evelyn over, and she joined me where I was leaning against the side of the building. Gesturing toward Olivia, she said, "Don't worry about her. She seems to be more interested in making the concert Instagram-worthy than in the concert itself." She looked at me and raised an eyebrow. "So, that Madison performance went well."

I winced. "Okay, so she got a little stage fright. She found her footing eventually."

"After her biggest fan turned up out of the blue with all the words to her song? You can't count on that happening again in August."

"I'm not giving up on her that easily. Who knows how much

31

she's capable of if we just give her a chance?"

Evelyn sighed. "I don't work in the music industry, Bailey, but even I know that you have to be comfortable in front of a crowd if you want to be a performer. You can't turn someone into something they're not." A wistful look crossed her face. "Remember how natural you were in front of an audience? It was like you truly became yourself the second you stepped onstage. You were radiant. And everyone in the crowd fed off that light and energy. You didn't even have to try."

I looked up at the smattering of stars in the darkened sky, trying to find the girl that Evelyn remembered. I glanced over at my friend and, in a voice so soft it hardly registered, asked, "Do you remember how happy we were back then?"

Her eyes were wary as they probed my face. "Of course I do. But you must have new reasons to be happy now, right? It's been six years."

Her question laid bare all the things that had changed since then. I opened my mouth and closed it right away as I realized it was all too much to put into words.

I looked in the vague direction of my hometown and ran a hand through my hair. "I don't even know why I decided to come back to Oak Plains. Being there just reminds me of how different everything is now."

"I know why you came back."

I turned to face my friend. "What do you mean?"

"You still have hope that things will change, even if you don't want to admit it to yourself. I know you like to think you've changed so much over the past few years, but I know you, Bailey. You're not ready to give up yet." She gave a small smile. "You're more like your sister than you think. I've always said that optimism runs in your family."

I turned over her words in my mind. Was I still holding out hope? A part of me was, perhaps, but I'd become so good at extinguishing any spark of hope that I couldn't tell if it had ever really existed. At the same time, maybe Evelyn was right. Maybe I wasn't all that different from the woman who used to thrive on hope and optimism. The thought both terrified me and made it a little easier to breathe.

"I can't get my hopes up again. You saw what that did to me."

"It wasn't getting your hopes up that made you this way. It was abandoning hope. Remember when you took that production assistant job after moving to Ackerdale? You tried to tell yourself that you were living the life you used to dream about when you were a music major in college. But you knew you weren't. You weren't focusing on your own music at all. You were watching musicians perform every night while your own guitar sat in a dusty corner of your closet. Sure, it wasn't easy when you first graduated and worked two jobs trying to put your music out there, but at least you believed in yourself and your art."

I fixed my gaze on Evelyn, as if that would protect me from the sting of her words. "That production assistant job *saved* me, Ev. Having a routine kept me sane. Otherwise, I would've kept ruminating on everything that went wrong that summer."

She gave me a thoughtful look. "Maybe it's good you're here, then. You're going to have to face the past eventually. And once you do, I have a feeling you'll get past this funk you're in."

Before I could tell her not to count on that, Olivia appeared at her side. "Can we *please* go now?"

"Sure, sweetie. Just let me say goodbye to Bailey, okay?" Evelyn turned and smiled at me. "Good to see you again. Call me if you need anything, okay?"

I nodded, wondering if she'd said that because she was secretly worried about how things would turn out for me now that I'd returned to Oak Plains. Despite her encouraging words, Evelyn had always been more realistic than my sister. She saw things for what they were. If anyone understood that happy endings weren't always possible, it was Evelyn. As much as I loved Cassidy, she was usually too blinded by her rose-colored glasses to see the world the way I did.

I stood there alone long after Evelyn walked off to her car with Olivia's whining accompanying her. All the energy I'd expended trying to keep hope at bay had only amplified its presence inside me, and I couldn't stop repeating Evelyn's words in my mind: *I know you, Bailey. You're not ready to give up yet.* She, of all people, should know better. I hadn't had a reason to be hopeful in years. Besides, if I let the feeling in now, it was bound to abandon me when things inevitably went awry. And the fall would be profoundly painful when it did.

I'd seen this movie too many times, and I was tired of watching the car crash into the building. I knew it was going to happen; I just didn't know when. And perhaps the worst part of it all was not knowing.

I took slow, heavy steps back to my car, as if I were wading through mud. After driving out of the parking lot, I turned on the radio and raised the volume until I could no longer hear my own thoughts.

Chapter 4

I was halfway through a call with Madison's agent on Saturday afternoon, trying to get an interview with the singer, when the yelling began from somewhere in the house. I pressed a finger to my ear to block it out, but it only escalated. Even though I'd escaped to the second-floor study to make my phone call in relative peace, Leah and Jade's argument sounded like it was taking place just outside the door.

"Mom promised she would take me to the petting zoo! You can go to the mall another time!"

"I need a new dress for Amanda's party this Friday. That's way more important than your stupid games."

"*Mom*! Jade just called me stupid!"

"That's not what I said! You never listen to me!"

"Dad, tell Mom she promised!"

"You're such a whiny baby! Just go to your dumb petting zoo, okay?"

My face burned as silence filtered through on the other end of the phone line. "Can I call you back later? I'm so sorry."

Madison's agent assured me it was fine in an unconvincing tone, and I thanked her before setting down my phone in defeat. I rubbed my temples as Eric's reprimanding voice cut through the girls' heated dispute. How was anyone supposed to hear their thoughts in this house?

When I reached the bottom of the stairs, a smug Leah was heading out the door while a sulky Jade retreated to her room. Eric threw me an apologetic look. "Sorry about that. When those two go at it, it can be hard to stop them."

"No worries. I was just about to head out anyway."

"All right, well, enjoy the weather. Looks like it's turning out to be a glorious day."

He was right, I learned as I stepped out into the bright afternoon. It was the perfect excuse to go for a long drive with no real destination. I got into my car and turned on the local country radio station before heading onto the main road.

Jason Aldean's "Dirt Road Anthem" came on as I passed by the ranch that Cassidy and I had visited as kids. Peering out at the sprawling green pasture, I watched the horses traverse the space, several of them stopping to graze on the grass every now and then. Even though the two of us had taken our turns riding the horses, Cassidy always convinced me that she had been born on a saddle. I could never bring myself to trust the animal like my sister did. In a small, dark part of me, I couldn't help but wonder if that same lack of trust was behind my reluctance to accept any joy into my life.

I was tempted to wallow in the thought, but I couldn't deprive myself of the simple pleasure of a scenic drive on a beautiful day. So I turned my attention to Jason's smooth, deep voice and made a point of setting aside my concerns for another time.

I drove aimlessly for a while, not stopping until I reached a dead end on Marigold Drive. There, I made a U-turn and headed back in the direction I came. The appeal of an aimless drive had worn off, and a Tide commercial replaced the country music that had been funneling out of the speakers. Every sign was pointing toward home. Yet as I neared the front yard of Cassidy's house, I found myself going in the complete opposite direction.

I continued forward, not knowing where I planned to end up until the Cooper Hardware sign came into view. I hesitated in front of the parking lot, not yet sure what I wanted to do but knowing I had to do it. Without a second thought, I pulled into an empty space and cut the engine. There was no turning back now.

Whatever force had propelled me toward the store seemed to take over my legs as I walked up and down the aisles. They kept going, not slowing down until I rounded the corner and spotted him by the power drills.

"Hi," I said to his back, as if I'd been planning to meet him here all along.

Dustin turned to face me, and a slow, easy smile spread across his face, sending fiery sparks through me. "Twice in one week? Must be a pretty big home improvement project you're workin' on."

I scanned the shelves frantically, trying to act like I understood the labels. "Uh… I need a hammer drill?" It took me a moment to notice that the shelf above the label was bare, and I mentally kicked myself.

He raised his eyebrows in amusement. "Why don't we head on over to the back and see if there are any extras?"

I followed him to the back room without comment. I felt a bit lightheaded, as if I was running a marathon in midsummer heat, and I was sure my heart had already skipped several beats. When was the last time I'd eaten something? Those corn flakes I'd found at the back of Cassidy's pantry had likely passed through my digestive tract hours ago.

Dustin sat down on an overturned crate in the far back of the room and looked up at me. "So, you wanna tell me the real reason you're here?"

To avoid answering the question, I tossed him an offended glance. "How do you know I don't need a hammer drill?"

"I don't. But if you did need one, you probably would've said it with more conviction."

Silence filled the small space, and I pretended to be engrossed in the pliers that hung on the wall opposite us. "Bailey, it's a Saturday afternoon. It's seventy-five degrees outside. I'm sure you have a million other places you could be right now." He smiled. "Don't get me wrong though. I'm glad you're here."

Before I could stop myself, I blurted, "Something just brought me here. I don't even know what it was. It just…" I slowly lifted my eyes to his. "It just felt like I had to be here."

"Well, maybe you shouldn't fight it." He took a step toward me, and I instinctively drew back, as if struck. My heart sank as I caught the hurt in his face.

"I'm sorry," I stammered. "I don't want to fight it anymore. I really don't. But I don't think I know how to just let go anymore."

He shook his head and said under his breath, "Well, ain't that the saddest thing I've ever heard you say."

For a moment, Dustin studied my face intently, like he was about to unearth an incredible discovery from my features. Just as I started to squirm under his gaze, he walked out of the back room and relayed some information to another employee. When he reappeared, he started walking toward the back door that led outside. "Come on. I think it's time."

"Time for what?"

He didn't respond. I followed him outside without protest, as if the same unknown force that had brought me to him was still overriding any sense of reason inside me. I was silent as he opened the passenger door of his Chevy pickup and waited for me to climb inside. I obeyed, sliding into the cab like it was the most natural thing in the world.

As he started the engine and backed out of the parking lot, I had the sudden urge to flip on the radio and blast whatever song came on. Anything to drown out the sound of my racing heart. He was sitting far too close to me not to hear it. I stole covert glances at him every now and then, wondering if he would ask me if I needed a glass of water. Or a sedative.

After about five minutes of driving, I couldn't help myself. I turned to him. "Where are we going?"

He kept his eyes focused on the road. "You'll find out soon enough."

A mile later, we stopped moving. I looked out the window and saw that we were parked on Acorn Lane. I turned to Dustin. "Why are we on my street?"

"Just go with the flow, Bailey."

I tried to conceal my frustration and followed him out of the truck. An uneasy feeling was blooming in my stomach, and it seemed to know what was coming before I did. After passing Cassidy's house and a couple houses next to it, Dustin strolled up to a lawn that had seen better days. The yellowed grass looked like it hadn't received proper maintenance in years, leaving stubborn weeds to sprout up in all directions. Oak trees craned their gnarled necks toward the grass in a vain attempt to revive it. Even the sun hanging in the sky looked paler than it did throughout the rest of town, as if it had already given up on nourishing the land that lay beneath it.

Before I could stop myself, my gaze drifted toward the mailbox. The only survivor of the fire. There it stood, cracked and faded from years of disuse but still bearing the three numbers I'd proudly printed every time I provided my address: *245.*

All the oxygen that my lungs had been holding whooshed out in a sudden gush, and my knees grew weak under the weight of the memories that were suffocating me. I turned in the other direction in what I could only describe as a survival instinct. "No way. I'm not going over there."

"You can't keep avoiding it," he said patiently. "You told me you wanted to let go, but you won't be able to do that if you keep holding on to the past. I know it's hard. But facing this is the first step you have to take."

I almost pointed out that those weren't my exact words, but he was right. I did want to let go. I wanted to run through the woods like the free spirit I used to be, wanted to soak up the sun's rays like they were only beating down on me. The more time I spent in this town, the more it seemed possible that I could be that girl again, despite how far I'd drifted from her.

But I was too afraid to see what lay beyond the thick mass of trees and unkempt lawn. Was it the same empty pit it had been after the firefighters cleaned up the debris? Or was a different family in the process of rebuilding a brand-new home? I wasn't sure which scenario would be a bigger slap to the face: seeing that absolutely nothing had changed since that horrific night or learning that a happy family had staked its claim on the property that used to be my haven.

"Is someone living there now?" I asked quietly. For a second, I reassured myself that Cassidy would have told me if someone had built a new home here. But she knew how sensitive the subject was for me, and I could just as easily understand her omitting that information entirely.

Dustin took a step back, making room for me to cross the invisible threshold. "There's only one way to find out."

I took slow, wary steps past the mailbox while Dustin followed closely behind me. I let out a small gasp when my eyes landed on a perfectly untouched lawn, as if the fire had never happened. A breathless sound like a trapped sob floated out of me. As I lowered myself onto the itchy carpet of grass, the sob broke free. Hot streaks of tears that were six years overdue painted my face. Right behind the pain was a sense of catharsis that I'd missed out on all these years. Back then, my shock-ridden self hadn't brought herself to cry. But now that I had, I realized the tears I'd trapped inside me all this time had been suffocating me.

Dustin sat down beside me and stroked my hair in slow, soothing motions. It struck me that I didn't feel too self-conscious to cry in front of him. I felt safe around him in a way I felt with very few people in my life. It was a deep-seated understanding that I wasn't judged in his presence but rather understood.

After I'd calmed down a bit, Dustin said, "It's okay to cry. It's the only way you heal."

"I think I'm six years too late," I murmured.

"There's no rush. Only you know how much time you need 'til you can move on."

After taking a deep breath, I said, "So, no one has even thought about rebuilding yet?"

He shook his head. "I'm sure it's crossed some folks' minds, but no one's actually done anything. Everyone saw how devastated you were after what happened. They've left the land alone out of respect for you and your family."

I felt my heart swell with love for the town I'd turned my back on all this time. While I'd been selfishly marinating in my own grief, the people of Oak Plains had never stopped caring about me.

We sat in peaceful silence for a minute. I watched as Dustin looked out at the trees that towered over us. His faded blue jeans and Braves hat reminded me of the southern boy he'd once been. I wondered if he was remembering those days, looking at the landscape and comparing it to the one that he used to call home.

"Do you ever miss Georgia?" I asked him.

His reflective expression took on a somber note. "Sometimes. Mostly when I'm fishing down by the creek or driving past the farms. But I love it here even if I have to put up with the brutal Northeast winters."

"Why did you leave?"

His somber expression turned a shade darker. "My mom died when I was thirteen, and my dad couldn't stand to be in the same town without her. He needed a fresh start. We all did. He had a good friend up in Philly, so he moved us out there. But city living wasn't for him. Didn't take long for him to start looking into smaller towns where he wouldn't be too far away from nature. After a while, he settled on Oak Plains. Then he opened his hardware store here, and the rest is history."

"I'm so sorry about your mom," I said. It was the widest he'd opened the door of his past for me so far, and I trod carefully around what I knew was a sensitive topic. "And just picking up and moving out here… That must've been a big adjustment for all of you."

"It was. But this is my home now. I can't imagine what life would be like if I never moved here." He peered into my face. "That's what I've been trying to tell you. Things might not be the way they used to be, but you can't waste your time wishing they were different. It's up to you to make the most of what you have now."

"Is that why you brought me here?"

He nodded. "But I also wanted to show you that you can still move on, even when you're standing right in the middle of the past."

"You say it like it's easy."

"It ain't easy, trust me. But I see that fight inside you, and I know it's tellin' you not to give up."

I studied his open, kind face and felt my guard slowly coming down. I suddenly wanted him to know everything I'd been keeping locked inside of me. I drew in a breath, knowing I needed to start somewhere. "I still blame myself for what happened that night. I know deep down that my family forgives me and that they moved on a long time ago. But I haven't. It's like I'm forever stuck in that moment after the music stopped, reliving the guilt over and over again."

"But that's just it. The only person who still hasn't forgiven you is yourself. And you need that forgiveness from yourself more than anyone else."

Picking at a limp blade of grass by my feet, I said, "I haven't sung or even touched my guitar in years. And I mostly listen to music for work these days. I rarely do it on my own time."

"Where do you work?"

"Mountain Lion Records. It's an indie country label in Pittsburgh. I'm an A&R coordinator, so I spend most of my time looking for new talent. Which is why I've been busy putting together a lineup for the concert."

"You mean you're not performing this year?"

I averted my gaze like a student who'd just been chastised by her teacher. "No."

He gave a low whistle. "This is much worse than I thought."

After considering me for a moment, he rose from his spot on the grass and tapped a few times on his phone. He glanced at me. "What kinda music you in the mood for?"

I remembered listening to "Dirt Road Anthem" on the way to the hardware store and decided I wanted more of that laid-back, country-rock sound. "Jason Aldean."

Dustin smiled as he put on "You Make It Easy." As he walked toward me, he said, "If I'm going to do one thing right this summer, it's helping you find your love for music again. You're not the Bailey I know if you're not singing or playin' guitar."

As Jason sweetened the air with his honeyed lyrics, Dustin placed his hands in mine. Something surged through my system at his touch, and it felt like every nerve ending in my body was charged with electricity. I tried to pull away, but it was impossible to detach myself from him, to quiet the blaze that was raging inside me.

"This is how we do it in Georgia," he said. With our fingers still intertwined, he twirled me around and pulled me close to him. Right there in the middle of the lawn where my demolished home once stood, we danced. Somehow, my feet fell into the right rhythm without me having to try. We were so close that my nose tingled with the woodsy scent emanating from him, and I could almost feel his beard grazing my face.

The proximity of him was making me lose my balance, and I was certain he noticed. In a weak attempt at humor, I said, "I'm not sure how we do it in Pennsylvania, but apparently this is it."

He laughed, causing the tension in my shoulders to melt away. I let myself relax and moved naturally in time with the music. "You're doin' just fine," he said.

The song reached the chorus, and Dustin twirled me around again. The absurdity of what we were doing wasn't lost on me. The guy who used to sit next to me in math class was dancing with me. In the middle of the day. To a cheesy country song that was piping out of his tinny phone speaker.

It all seemed so ridiculous in that moment that I started to laugh. Dustin smiled. "What is it?"

"All of this," I said, gesturing broadly. "What we're doing right now." I shook my head and smiled. "If it were anyone else, I'd think they were crazy. But you somehow make this feel like the most natural thing in the world."

He grinned. "Crazy enough that you'll think of me serenading you country-style every time you drive past here?"

I laughed again, and his eyes sparkled in the sunlight. "You know your laugh is my second favorite sound in the world, right?"

"What's your favorite?"

"Your singing voice." As his arms circled my waist, Dustin looked deep into my eyes. "Sing, Bailey. I want to hear your voice again."

Just as swiftly as my muscles unclenched, they tensed up again. "I can't."

"Sure you can."

I staggered backward. "I should get going. My sister's

probably wondering where I am."

A teasing smile danced on his lips. "Sure, but don't forget you left your car in the parking lot at the store."

Silently cursing my forgetfulness, I crossed my arms over my chest. Dustin seemed to sense that I was closing myself off and blew out a frustrated breath. After staring at the ground for a moment, he raised his eyes to me again. "I won't make you sing if you're not ready. But just know that I'm not giving up until you are."

He led me to his truck while a deep fondness for him rose inside me. He didn't try to coax me to do anything I didn't feel comfortable doing. He embraced me for who I was, even when that was a mess of tears and painful memories. It was everything I didn't know I'd needed all this time.

After he drove me back to the store, I got in my car and headed to Cassidy's house in silence. The afternoon came back to me in waves during the entire ride. I felt as if I'd woken up from a strange sort of dream, one where the details were abnormally vivid. The newness of it all made me fear that it would disappear just as quickly as it had come into my life. The way he made me feel was too good to be true. Surely something that pure and beautiful had to be a figment of my imagination.

I was a little unsteady on my feet as I let myself into the foyer. Cassidy started to greet me, then slightly squinted her eyes. "You okay there, Bailey? You look a little flushed."

"I'm fine. It's just really hot out."

"You were gone a while."

"I was just driving around the countryside. Taking in the views." I poked my head into the kitchen and sniffed with more force than was necessary. "Are you making pot roast? It smells heavenly."

She raised an eyebrow but didn't push any further. I gave the universe a silent thank you for letting me off the hook this time.

Half an hour later, we all sat down for dinner—me, Cassidy, Eric, and the kids. I glanced down at my steaming plate of food and felt my stomach churn. When Cassidy had first met Eric, she couldn't eat for days. "Now it's happening to me," I muttered to my mashed potatoes.

Eric looked up from his plate. "Did you say something?"

I jerked my head up to see that the entire table was staring at me. I shook my head. "No."

Before anyone could respond, Leah sat up in her chair. "Who wants to hear what happened at the petting zoo?"

"Literally no one," Jade said.

Ignoring her sister, Leah launched into a long-winded story about forging a friendship with one of the sheep while I only listened with one ear. I was too overwhelmed with gratitude that my younger niece had successfully redirected the spotlight to herself.

That didn't last long enough. The second Leah ran out of steam, Cassidy eyed my cold pot roast. "You haven't touched your food."

I poked the juicy slab of meat with my fork. "I'm not that hungry."

"You seemed pretty excited to eat when you dove into the kitchen earlier."

I shot her a look, but she didn't drop her expectant gaze. The look on her face told me she was channeling the sixth sense that we'd always shared as sisters. I didn't even have to ask to know she was reading my thoughts like the open page of a magazine.

"Mom, is Aunt Bailey sick?" Leah asked.

"No, honey." Cassidy's eyes locked with mine. "Just lovesick."

I nearly choked on my water, sending tiny droplets splattering onto my napkin. Cassidy's eyes were smiling, and I wanted to slap her for it. She was responsible for sending me down this path of false hope. She'd known what that first trip to the hardware store would mean, but she'd assigned me the errand anyway.

"Oh no! Aunt Bailey is choking!" Leah turned to Eric in a panic. "Dad can save her! He's TPR certified!"

"It's CPR, dumbass," Jade said.

"Jade." Eric shot his daughter a stern look. "Don't talk to your sister like that."

Their squabble created the perfect distraction, so I picked up my plate and stood to leave. "I'm fine," I reassured Leah. "I just need to lie down for a bit."

I made a point of avoiding Cassidy's eyes as I put my plate in the sink and headed upstairs. Once I was ensconced in the safety of the guest room, I lay down on the bed and stared up at the ceiling. Whatever this was, I had to put a stop to it. I'd let myself soar too high that afternoon, had let happiness make itself too comfortable in my heart. Now, I was hanging on the edge of a precipice, waiting for the plummet to come at any moment.

It wasn't worth making myself vulnerable again. Not when I knew exactly how this story was going to end. It was easier not to fling myself onto a path that was bound to leave me disappointed.

At the same time, I'd already done it. I'd stepped onto that path the second he'd uttered my name in the hardware store. Whatever had just happened on the lawn had only sucked me deeper into the tornado that was whirling around me.

I turned on my side and stared out at the slice of sky through the window. As much as I knew that I was taking a big risk, and that I should back out now while I still could, I didn't want to. The same part of me that wanted to run full speed in the other direction also ached to run just as quickly toward him until I had safely landed in his arms. And to never let go once I was there.

I flipped onto my back again and fixed my gaze on the ceiling. "Damn you, Dustin Cooper," I muttered under my breath.

Chapter 5

Lauren needed me in the office Monday morning, so I made the three-hour journey to the Mountain Lion Records headquarters in Pittsburgh. Lauren claimed that my interview with Madison needed to take place in a professional environment, but I knew the only reason she wanted me there was because I'd already been away from the office for longer than planned.

I'd barely settled into my office when Lauren clopped toward my desk. She was wearing a pinstripe blouse and had pulled back her blond hair into a tight ponytail. I'd been working for her long enough to know that look only meant business.

"Hey," she said, slightly out of breath. "Madison should be here any minute now. Do you have your questions ready?"

I patted the notebook beside me. "All taken care of."

"Good." She started to turn around but stopped and faced me again. "I'm sorry. How are you? I haven't seen you since you brought over your sister's cornbread. It was delicious, by the way."

I smiled. "I'm doing okay. And I'll be sure to pass that on to her."

She studied me for a moment. "You look… different. Happier, I think."

At a loss for words, I said, "Well, it's been nice seeing my family again. And my hometown." I didn't mention Dustin, the elephant in the room that only I could see.

"Sounds like it." She stole a glance at my notebook. "Don't be afraid to dig deep during the interview. We're going to be signing the best artist who performs at your summer concert, so just think about who has the most selling potential."

I nodded as she turned and walked away, but her previous comment was still echoing through my mind. *Happier, I think.* People were beginning to notice. My contentment was no longer a private understanding between me and my heart. It had begun to seep out of my features and leak out of my voice, exposing the way the fog over my soul had lifted for the first time in years. Now that it was a real, tangible thing, I could feel its presence lingering in the air around me. And that only made me more aware of its fleeting nature.

Before I could spend another second dwelling on my feelings, a petite woman with long, caramel hair and tanned skin appeared in the doorway beside Danielle, the receptionist. "I have Madison Brenner here to see you."

"Thanks, Danielle." I waved Madison over to my desk. "Come on in."

She took a tentative step into my office and sat on the chair opposite me. "I'm really excited to be here," she said emphatically, as if to cover up her evident anxiety.

I smiled. "I'm glad. I saw you perform this past weekend, and you definitely have talent. I just hope we can focus a little more on the talent and less on the nerves."

At the mention of the concert, she blanched. I felt a twinge of empathy for her. Most people in my position wouldn't give her a second chance after her slipup. But, somehow, I saw beyond that. I saw something inside her that kept me from giving up on her. Maybe I was one of the few who recognized that underneath her veneer of shyness was hunger. She wanted this. Even more, I suspected, than those wannabe superstars whose exaggerated confidence concealed their lack of natural musical talent.

"I know you're thinking of what went wrong at that show, but what matters to me is that you got back on your feet. Most people would've let that derail them. You didn't though. I know you can use that spunk to get to where you want to be."

Just like that, she was beaming. It was as if I'd fed water to a wilting flower. Now that she seemed to be in better spirits, I opened my notebook and started scanning the questions I'd jotted down. Before I could speak, Madison's eyes widened at something behind me. "What's that?"

I turned around and saw what had captured her attention. Framed on the wall behind my desk was a blown-up image of my first and only album cover. Evelyn had taken the photo after we'd driven around town in search of a worthy backdrop. Somewhere along the way, I'd gotten distracted by a field of wildflowers in a desolate area off the highway. As I wandered through the fresh blossoms, Evelyn snapped a candid picture of me in a state of unfiltered awe. The image captured the mood of my album so perfectly that I'd ended up choosing it for the cover artwork.

"It's just an album I recorded a while back," I said, scanning the title that was emblazoned across the photo: *Wanderlust*. "It never hit the Billboard charts or anything. It was just a little project I did for fun."

"You recorded an album? Like, in a professional studio?"

"Kind of. My friend knew someone who worked at a studio, and he taught me the ropes of the recording process. But I wasn't tied to a label or anything."

Madison was still entranced by my album cover. "You sure look like you were having fun."

Ignoring the pang in my chest, I glanced down at my notes. "We should get started on the questions now." I eyed the first one I'd written down. "In your opinion, what can you bring to the music industry that no one else…"

My voice trailed off as I noticed the question in Madison's eyes. "Is something wrong?"

"It's just…" She cocked her head, as if deep in thought. "You seem so much more serious now. It's kind of hard to believe that's you in the picture."

I felt my face redden, and I couldn't help but wonder how our roles had reversed. She was the one who was supposed to be sweating. Not me.

"I'm at work now. Not exactly a fair comparison, don't you think?" My tone was sterner than I intended, but that was the only way I would stop her from prying any further. I was beginning to regret having displayed that picture in the center of the wall.

"Do you still make music?" Madison asked, undeterred by my tone. The girl seemed to get a confidence boost from putting me on the spot.

I gave a short chuckle. "Shouldn't I be the one asking the

questions here?" But it only took a quick glance at her face to see that she wasn't ready to back down yet.

I sighed and set my palms on my desk. "I'm going to cut right to the chase, okay? My hometown holds a big concert every August, and we're anticipating that it'll have an even bigger turnout this summer. Anyone who wants to become somebody would be lucky to be up on that stage. I was going to offer you a spot, but I want to make sure you're serious about this first. So, as much as I love chatting about my own musical past, I'm only interested in yours right now."

Her eyes lit up in recognition. "You mean the one in Oak Plains? My family used to take me there all the time. I grew up in Hayestown, so I was right next door to you."

I looked at her in genuine shock. "Really?" I remembered reading that she was from Hayestown, but it hadn't occurred to me that she might have attended the summer event.

She nodded. "The last time I went was about six years ago, when I was fifteen or so. This poor girl was singing her heart out, having the time of her life, and then she just froze. Like, *bam*. I don't know if she forgot the lyrics or had a sudden case of stage fright, but she just stopped singing and ran off. I felt so sorry for her."

My mouth had dried up completely, and any words I wanted to say were wisps of cotton on my tongue. "I thought of that performance when I forgot the lyrics last weekend," Madison continued. "It reminded me that we're all human, and it's okay to mess up every now and then. It gave me hope, in a way." After a thoughtful pause, she said, "It's sad that she never performed again. If she got back up on that stage and redeemed herself, at least there would be a happy ending. Because I need to know that things can turn out okay after something that traumatizing

54

happens."

I blinked at the girl sitting in front of me, unable to form words. When I'd bolted off that stage, the only thing on my mind had been the state of my home. I'd been too wrapped up in my agony to consider the possibility that I wasn't the only one whose heart had been broken. That somewhere in the crowd, an aspiring singer like I'd once been was watching me, depending on me to possess the courage she couldn't find.

I rearranged some stray papers on my desk, no longer able to look Madison in the eye. "I'm sure she's doing better now. Just because you didn't see the happy ending doesn't mean there wasn't one."

As I watched a small smile brighten her face, I felt like a fraud. There was no happy ending, of course. But I couldn't bring myself to tell her that. Instead, I went ahead with the interview, moving on as if everything was business as usual. I knew deep inside, though, that the questions I was asking were just a formality. I owed it to her to give her a spot on the concert set list. And if I had to help her find her confidence, it would be a long overdue favor.

When the interview was over, I stopped by Lauren's office to let her know I'd chosen Madison as one of the performers. She raised her eyebrows at the news. "That was a quick decision."

"I have a gut feeling about her. Trust me."

I made my way back to my desk, satisfied with my choice. But for the rest of the morning, I couldn't stop thinking about how Madison would have reacted if I'd told her that girl had been me.

* * *

When I pulled up to Cassidy's driveway that evening, the faint sound of a child's laughter rippled through the air. I got out of the car and wandered toward the garden gate that led to the backyard. As I stepped onto the lawn, I saw Leah darting across the grass to catch the baseball Eric had thrown her. Her gloved hand shot up into the air just as the ball descended toward her, and she slid across the lawn, cupping the ball in her palm. "Got it!" she yelled victoriously.

Eric clapped as Leah rose to her feet. "Perfect job, Leah." He looked over at me. "Aunt Bailey agrees, right?"

"I sure do. That was impressive." I smiled as my niece gave a small bow for her two spectators. "The athletic gene must have skipped over me completely."

"Well, you've more than made up for it with your musical talent," Eric said.

Blushing, I turned my attention back to Leah. Watching her play in the beautiful weather reminded me of how Cassidy and I used to spend hours outside as kids, soaking up as much of the summer as we could before we returned to the confining classroom walls. I looked up at the cloudless sky and decided it wasn't too late to recreate one of those days with my sister. With everything that had been pressing down on my mind lately, I longed for one of our chats on the front porch that always helped sort out my thoughts better than any journal could.

"Do you know where Cassidy is?" I asked Eric.

"She had to run a few errands, but she should be back soon."

"Thanks." I smiled and waved goodbye to Leah as I headed into the house. "Keep up the good work, sweetie."

In the kitchen, I poured two tall glasses of iced tea and brought them out to the front porch. I set them down on the wicker table in between the two chairs and sat down on one of them.

While I waited for Cassidy to return, I peered across the street at our neighbors' cottage. The pale-yellow paint had begun to peel with time, and the darkened windows gave the impression that the house had been abandoned for a long time. I wondered absently if the same couple still lived there. While most Oak Plains residents laid down roots here and stayed well into their older years, it wasn't uncommon for people to wander off elsewhere in search of something more.

The sound of tires on the driveway pried me away from my thoughts. Cassidy pulled up in her truck and stepped out with a shopping bag in each hand. As she ascended the front steps, she blinked at me. "I'm sorry. I just need to make sure this isn't a mirage."

"You know I used to love sitting on the porch."

"*Used to* being the operative words."

I didn't feel like fighting her, so I just patted the other chair. "Can we talk for a minute? I brought out some iced tea. Your favorite."

She still looked suspicious as she put down her bags and sat beside me. She took a long sip of her beverage and met my eyes. "So, what's up?"

I suddenly couldn't bring myself to say what was really on my mind, so I eyed the cottage across the street. "Do Ruth and Craig still live there?"

She gave me a curious look. "Ruth does. Craig died a couple years ago. But I highly doubt that's the reason you wanted to talk."

"Maybe I just wanted to have some quality bonding time with my sister."

The corners of her mouth twitched like she was trying not to laugh. "That's really the best you could come up with?"

I crossed my arms. "My acting skills are a little rusty right now."

"They always have been. Just like they were at dinner on Saturday." She pulled her knees up to her chest and tilted her head at me. "Wanna tell me who that was all about?"

"You assume it's a who."

"Come on, Bailey. No one stares at their pork with a dreamy look in their eyes unless there's a man involved."

I didn't respond, and she began ticking off names on her fingers. "There's Logan from church, who went through quite the transformation last summer... Cole from the ranch—I heard he and his girlfriend broke up a few months ago... Let's see, who else..." She stopped and sat up straight. "Oh my God."

I didn't even have to ask who'd crossed her mind. "I'm officially leaving this conversation."

She clasped both my hands in hers and grinned. "It's Dustin, isn't it? I knew you two would end up together someday. I just had a gut feeling—"

"See, this is why I didn't want to tell you." I yanked my hands free from hers, and her entire face fell. It reminded me of Dustin's wounded expression when I pulled away from him at the hardware store. My eyes dropped to the patio floor, and I bit my lip to contain the tears. "I'm sorry. It's just that... I can't let something happen between us if it's only going to let me down. It's already getting too real, and I feel like my brain hasn't had the chance to catch up with what I'm feeling. I can't let myself do this until I'm sure it's what I want."

"But that's the problem. You're overthinking it. Thoughts don't have a place in matters of the heart."

I didn't say anything at first. After a moment, I looked up at Cassidy. "He danced with me."

"He *danced* with you?"

I nodded. "He took me to the front lawn of our old house and played Jason Aldean and just started dancing with me. He said he wanted me to think of that instead of the bad memories I have." I smiled to myself. "It sounds ridiculous now, but it felt so natural in a way I can't explain."

She chuckled and shook her head. "Those southern boys have romance running through their veins, I swear."

"And he made me laugh. Harder than I've laughed in a long time." I looked down at my hands. "I felt like myself for once. It reminded me of how happy I used to be years ago—and how this will probably be taken away from me eventually, just like it was then."

I was silent for a minute as I took in the comforting sight of our street. Beside me, Cassidy sighed. "I'm going to tell you something you won't like, but just hear me out, okay?"

I faced her tentatively. "Go ahead."

"You always talk about how things will never be the same as they used to be. And you know what? They won't. You were a different person then. And I have a feeling you'll never be able to be that person again. Life just moves forward, Bailey. It's the way it goes."

"Gee, thanks for the pep talk." My voice had an edge to it, a shield covering the gaping hole that her harsh truth had burrowed into me.

"But you know what?" She looked into my eyes, past the barrier I'd constructed. "That doesn't mean you'll never be happy again. It'll just be different. And once you stop wishing for everything to go back to the way it was before the fire, you'll be able to appreciate what you have now."

After thinking for a second, I turned to my sister. "Remember when I used to stay up all night writing songs? I could hardly keep up with all the ideas that popped in my head. I miss what that felt like."

Cassidy studied me closely. "You never lost your passion for music, Bailey. You're the one who gave up on it. I don't know when you're going to stop punishing yourself for what happened that summer." Her eyes swung over to the lawn as she fell silent. Quietly, she said, "Have you ever thought that maybe you would feel better if you started writing songs again? Music has always helped you through all the hard times in life. Again, I'm not saying everything will magically go back to normal. But maybe you'll at least start to heal and create a new path forward, which is a heck of a lot better than staying trapped in the past forever."

In the peacefulness of the porch, I tried to conjure up an image in my mind—one I'd come to know well through the years. I pictured my fingers manipulating the cool steel strings of my acoustic guitar as I plucked out the first chords of my song. I pictured stepping up to the microphone, the modest silver cone rendering me vulnerable and fearless at the same time. I pictured the crowd, hanging onto my every lyric and note before erupting into applause at the conclusion of my performance. Somewhere in the mass of spectators was Evelyn, Cassidy, and my parents, their joy rippling through the crowd and inflating me with pride.

Could I do that again? Could I ever have that kind of experience again, the kind that took me outside of myself and into a feeling of completeness that nothing else could bring? The stubborn hope inside me insisted that I could, but my heart refused to open itself up to the possibility. Its doors were shuttered, the strings that held it together warped and frayed from stretching themselves too far with hope in the past.

"Just something to think about," Cassidy said. She stood and picked up her bags before making her way to the front door. "Oh, and by the way," she said, her hand resting on the doorknob. "If Dustin made you feel like yourself again, that's really saying something. Because you haven't been yourself in years."

Chapter 6

I lay on my bed two days later, listening to the newest talent that I'd scraped out of the dredges of the internet. Hell Frozen Over, a pop-punk band from Cleveland, had a markedly aggressive sound that reminded me of something Jade would listen to. Despite the label they'd assigned themselves, I would've categorized them as metal or hardcore instead.

I stared at the ceiling, trying to imagine the song pumping through the speakers at the summer concert. Because the event represented all kinds of genres, I wanted to branch out from the country music I usually listened to. But the heavy guitars and fast-paced drums had no place at such a breezy, laid-back event. My optimism was wearing thin. If I couldn't find a promising artist other than Madison, it wouldn't be a summer concert anymore. It would be her headliner.

A light knock broke through the crunch of electric guitars. I sat up on my bed and shut off the music. "Come in."

Jade stepped inside hesitantly. "What band was that?"

"Hell Frozen Over. They claim to be pop punk, but I'd peg them as some kind of nu-metal group."

"Never heard of them. But they sound pretty cool."

"You've probably never heard of ninety-nine percent of the artists I listen to for work." I smiled and patted the spot on the bed next to me. "Have a seat."

Once she was sitting down beside me, I asked, "So, how are you getting along with your mom?"

She rolled her eyes. "She's the worst."

"She's my sister, you know."

"But you guys are so different. You're so much more chill than her. I want to go to a concert, and she acts like it's the end of the world."

"She's only doing that because she loves you. If you were my daughter, I would probably act the same way."

Jade crossed her arms and stared out the window, her face a hardened shell. Watching her, I remembered how Cassidy had urged me to speak to her daughter, saying I reminded her of Jade in so many ways. I thought of how misunderstood I'd felt when I was thirteen and how my mother's insistence that I would grow out of it only made me feel more invalidated. What Jade needed more than ever was to know that her struggles weren't falling on deaf ears.

I turned to face my niece. "I know you won't believe me, but I used to be a lot like you when I was your age. I hid behind dark eyeliner and listened to loud rock music—not too different from what you listen to now. I remember thinking that the lyrics understood me better than anyone else did."

I had her attention now. "Really?"

"Yup." I chuckled. "At my eighth-grade dance, I walked in

wearing the frilly dress that Grandma insisted I wear. Then, when I was sure she was gone, I snuck into the bathroom and changed into a plaid miniskirt with Converse high-tops. I still haven't forgotten the look of abject horror on her face when she caught me. She came to pick me up early, and I didn't have time to change back into my dress. Not only did she ground me, but she hid all of my CDs until I promised to stop listening to that 'demonic' music. She was convinced it was influencing me."

Jade's eyes were wide. "Are you serious? Even Mom isn't that bad."

"No, she isn't. Believe me, there's way worse out there. And I know it can feel like your mom is trying to ruin your life, because that's how I felt too. But now I know she was doing it because she just wanted me to fit in. It was her way of showing she cared, even if it didn't seem like it at the time."

She looked like she wanted to believe me, so I offered up an encouraging smile. "Try to cut your mom some slack, okay? She's doing the best she can."

"I guess," she said halfheartedly. Knowing that was the best I was going to get from her, I smiled. "That's great to hear."

A drilling noise sliced through the window, making both Jade and me jump. I stood up and peered through the glass. The front lawn and our street looked as peaceful as ever, the view at odds with the harsh sound of the drill.

I turned and looked at Jade. "Where is that coming from?"
She shrugged.

Intrigued, I headed down the stairs and went out to the back porch, where the drilling grew louder. It wasn't until I was standing right in front of the swing set that I saw him drilling at the thick oak that held the tree house.

I shielded my eyes from the sun. "Dustin?"

He turned to me and smiled. I tried to forget about the sight of his strong, tanned arms working the drill and glared pointedly at the tree. "Who gave you permission to tear down the tree house?"

He raised an eyebrow. "I'm not tearing it down. I'm expanding it. Your sister wanted Leah to have more room to play inside it with her friends." With an amused look, he said, "You seem pretty worked up about it though."

The amount of trouble my sister went through just to put the two of us together was remarkable. I looked up at the tree house, nostalgia sweeping over me. It was an exact replica of the one that used to jut out from the dogwood tree in my childhood backyard. "This was one of my favorite places to hang out when I was a kid too. Leah will love the extra space."

Dustin jerked his head toward the tree house. "Some of your old toys are still in there. Thought you might like to see them before I finish up my work here."

A tiny gasp escaped me as I ascended the steps and saw what he was talking about. The tree house was dotted with dozens of knickknacks that sent me right back to my childhood. I smiled to myself as I peeked into the dollhouse and studied the miniature rooms that I'd furnished with Cassidy. Even as a young child, I had an eye for design.

"That was my favorite too," Dustin said. I started a bit as I turned and saw him sitting right behind me. He chuckled. "Didn't mean to startle you. You were really absorbed there for a minute."

The air in the small space felt too thick with him sharing it. I was hyperfocused on every movement his body made, of every feature on his face. Just as powerful as the desire to reach out and touch him was the urge to climb back down to the ground where I could find my breath again.

"So, do you have a day off from work or something?" I asked in what I hoped was a conversational tone.

He smiled. "This *is* my work, Bailey. I just step in at the store when my dad needs some extra help. But for the past five years or so, I've been the resident handyman in town. As long as there are tools involved, you can count on me being there." He reached over and picked up a purple felt microphone. "Kind of how I imagine you feel about singing."

I couldn't help but giggle at the sight of the toy microphone. "That brings back so many memories. I used to sing in my room with that microphone and pretend I was performing at a sold-out show. Cassidy and Evelyn were my only fans, of course."

"You had a lot more fans than that. Remember the way people would cheer for you at the summer concert?"

His comment reminded me of Madison saying she wished I would perform at the concert again. Between her and Cassidy, it seemed that everyone was rooting for me to get back up onstage. And, just like it did after my conversation with Cassidy, hope warmed my veins once again. This time, though, I let it stick around for a while. I let myself savor the feeling of it loosening the chains on my heart and shining a light into the crevices of my soul.

Without warning, I said, "I think I might start writing music again."

He looked genuinely surprised, and I thought I caught a glimpse of relief in his eyes as well. "Really? When did you make that decision?"

"It was sort of Cassidy's idea. It got me thinking about the whole process of making music and how I've missed it more than I thought. I'm not sure what I would write my next song about. I just know it's something I want to do again."

He didn't say anything at first, and I was sharply aware of the sound of my heart beating in the full-fledged silence. In a voice so soft I almost didn't hear it, he said, "Maybe you can write a song about this."

In the still air of the tree house, he kissed me, long and tenderly. Before my brain could get in the way, I closed my eyes and leaned into the kiss like a flower craning its stem toward the sun. It felt as natural as the dance we'd shared on my old front lawn. As our lips melded together, I couldn't help but think that this was what I'd been missing out on since we met in high school.

We pulled away slowly, and I bit my lip as I looked at him. "That would be quite the song," I said.

"I think so too." Running his fingers through my hair, he said, "I bet we could write a whole album together."

"I'd love that," I breathed.

He kissed me again, and I held him like his body was designed just for mine. My breaths grew ragged as his tongue explored my mouth. While I fumbled my way toward him, my foot grazed the hard plastic of a cowgirl Barbie doll, and the red heat of shame crept up my cheeks as I pictured my younger self witnessing this scene in her favorite hideout.

"Mom, there's someone in the tree house!"

We tore away from each other just as quickly as we'd fallen into each other's arms. Leah appeared at the top of the staircase, her eyes bulging at the sight of the two of us.

"What are you doing here?" I snapped.

"What are *you* doing here? This is my tree house." She stuck her tongue out at me by way of making her point.

Dustin smiled warmly at her. "I just stopped by to do some work on it. You remember me, right?"

"Of course! You're Mr. Cooper from the store."

"Atta girl!" He reached over to high-five Leah, who was beaming. As I watched him, I was overcome with an affection for him that was different from what I felt when we'd kissed. No matter whom he was with, whether it was me or my niece, he had a way of brightening their world with his mere presence. Warmth and light came as naturally to him as darkness did to a cave. Enough light, maybe, to fill the cracks in my heart and patch it up again.

"Mom wants to talk to you," Leah told Dustin. "She said it's important."

He exchanged a glance with me and said, "Tell her I'll be there in a minute."

"Okay," she said cheerily before descending the stairs. I'd never been more grateful that six-year-olds were oblivious to sexual tension.

"That was close," I muttered.

He chuckled. "Don't worry. I think she was more focused on the toys than us."

As if on cue, Leah's singsong voice floated up from the lawn. "Aunt Bailey and Mr. Cooper sittin' in a tree. K-I-S-S-I-N-G."

"Literally," Dustin muttered, the corners of his mouth fighting a grin.

I buried my beet-red face in my hands. "How am I ever going to go back down there?"

He gave up on holding back his smile. "Same way you came up, but backward."

I punched his arm, and he laughed. "Don't worry," he said.

Chapter 6

"She's six. She'll forget about it by tonight."

"My sister won't." I sighed, thinking of how pleased Cassidy must be with herself right now. "She definitely got her wish."

"She's not the only one, you know." He held his gaze on me for a moment before rising from the floor of the tree house. "Well, I don't want to keep Cassidy waiting. I'm pretty sure she's already noticed that I haven't been working for the past ten minutes."

I tamped down the disappointment rising inside me. I wanted to ask him about working at the store, about his goals, about every part of his life that mattered to him. I wanted to *know* him. And I had the feeling he wanted to know me too.

"By the way," he said before heading down the stairs, "I've wanted to do that since high school."

After he disappeared, I sat alone in the tree house, staring up at strips of blue sky from between the wood slats of the roof. The ghost of his kiss still lingered on my lips, and his invisible embrace warmed me like the sun's rays. It was a sensation that was familiar and novel at the same time. Out of all the kisses I'd had in my life, not a single one had ever felt like that.

I wasn't ready to go inside yet, so I headed down the tree house steps and moved to the front porch. I stayed there until the sunset faded to black, giving way to a clear night sky. Against the dark canvas, I saw all the highlights of my short time with him, as if I were looking at a photo reel. I closed my eyes, wanting to preserve them in the eye of my memory for as long as I could.

Cassidy opened the front door, breaking me out of my reverie. "Looking at the stars all by yourself? Well, that can only mean one thing."

I looked at her in a panic. "Did you hear Leah?"

"I'm pretty sure the whole town heard her. But don't worry." She flashed a smile. "This is what I've been cooking up ever since I asked him to come over."

"So, you didn't actually need work done on the tree house?"

She shrugged. "The project has been on my mind for a while. I just figured the romantic timing was right, if you know what I mean." She looked at me expectantly. "So, are you going to satisfy my hopeless romantic fantasies and tell me how amazing it was?"

"That I'm keeping to myself. But I actually wanted to tell you that you were right."

"About what?"

"About what you told me yesterday. That things will never be the same as they were before. They aren't the same at all, but I think that's the best part."

Smiling, she said, "I'm so glad you see that now."

I turned my eyes to the darkened lawn. "I can't believe he was there all along, you know? Ever since I was sixteen and he was seventeen. I never paid him any attention until now."

"I could tell he was interested in you back then. But you were too stuck in your own head to notice." Her expression sobered. "I remember when he found out you left Oak Plains. I'd never seen him so broken up before. He didn't show up at the store for weeks."

A lump lodged itself into my throat. "Really?"

She nodded. "He cares about you a lot. He was heartbroken about the fire too. It was like your pain became his own."

"I care about him too." I hadn't planned to say those words until they were out of my mouth, but now that they sat in the air around us, I knew they were the truth.

She gave my shoulder a little squeeze. "I know you do."

As we sat together in the still of the night, I thought back to what I'd said to Dustin before he kissed me. I looked at my sister and smiled. "You know, I had a little idea that I shared with him when we first went up to the tree house."

"Oh yeah? What was that?"

I hesitated before verbalizing my plan, like I needed to make sure it was what I really wanted first. But there was no more room for hesitation. I'd already been putting off this moment for far too long.

"I think I'm ready to start writing music again. Just to see how it feels," I added quickly.

Cassidy's eyes were gleaming. She jumped up from her chair and hugged me. "I knew you couldn't resist making music in this town." She looked down at me with a smug smile. "You're only one step away from getting back on that stage, you know."

"In your dreams."

"Then I'll keep dreaming until it comes true." She sat back down and looked at me impatiently. "Well, what you are you waiting for? Get busy. Your next big hit is ready."

I smiled and shook my head. "If I'd known you were going to be this excited, I would've whipped out my guitar a long time ago."

"You already know we've all been waiting for you to sing again. You're the only one who's stopped it from happening."

She was right. I *had* stopped it from happening. And now it was up to me to steer things in the opposite direction. To revive my voice after having silenced it for so long. Knowing I had the power to make that happen gave me the urge to start dancing right there on the porch.

I'd gotten it wrong all this time. I thought I'd been the one waiting for the music inside me to start playing again, but really, it had been the other way around. The invisible melody in my heart had been waiting patiently for me to hear it. And I was finally listening.

I turned to Cassidy with a gleam in my eye. "Do you still have my guitar?"

She beamed. "I thought you'd never ask."

I followed Cassidy into the house, where she headed up the stairs and turned into the guest room. She walked straight to the closet and rooted around in the back for my guitar. After a minute, she unearthed the instrument from a corner and held it up victoriously. My veins pulsed with excitement at the same time as sadness tightened my chest. It was hard to believe my treasured guitar still existed after everything that had changed since the last time I held it in my hands.

"Still in one piece," I said, my voice nearly a whisper.

"And waiting for you to make some magic with it." Cassidy handed me the instrument like she was bestowing superpowers upon me. "Enough chitchat. I'll let you do your thing."

She disappeared down the stairs while I marveled at the guitar like I was seeing it for the first time. After removing the thin layer of dust that had settled on the instrument, I sat on my bed and held it close to my chest. I could hear it speaking to me, translating the lyrics I had yet to write.

So much had happened since the fire that I failed to find a singular topic to focus on. The highlights of the past six years darted through my mind, as if I were watching them on fast forward. Somewhere among all the pain and joy was the perfect starting point for a song. I just needed to find it.

Gingerly, I strummed my first chord and let the sound occupy the space around me. Once I'd released the first note into the world, the second one came a little more easily. Then the third, then the fourth, and then I was playing an actual song. The feeling was so surreal, so pure and raw, that I found myself at the mercy of the instrument in my hands. I fought to keep up with the song that was writing itself, the melody breaking free from deep within me.

Once the song was in motion, I paused and wandered over to the study in search of notebook paper. I used to document all of my lyrics in the songbook I'd lost in the fire. That small leather-bound book had never left my side. I snuck a verse or two in there everywhere I went, whether it was the college lecture hall or my favorite restaurant. Even now, I felt the loss just as sharply as I had that night.

I let out a breath and pushed the memories aside. I'd just started composing my first song in years. That meant it was time to move forward, not backward. I pulled a spiral notebook out of the desk drawer and ripped out a blank sheet of paper. After carrying the paper and a pen to the guest room, I closed the door behind me and settled back on the bed.

I scribbled down the title that had been echoing through my mind while I played: "Different This Time." Nearly everything in my life had changed since the last time I was in Oak Plains. The only fixed variable was the town itself. But, as Cassidy had helped me understand, different didn't have to mean worse. In fact, the complete opposite could be true. As long as I stopped comparing the present to the past, I could enjoy where I was now without constantly looking behind me.

I went with the flow and played as the words came to me. I made room for everything that I'd gone through over the past few years, starting with that August night and ending with my return to my hometown. It was a mix of the good and the bad, with more of an emphasis on the good.

When I reviewed what I'd written, I was pleased to notice that I'd ended my song on a hopeful note. It was a common theme of my music—so much so that Evelyn enjoyed teasing me for not having the guts to write a sad song. It made me wonder if she was right when she'd pointed out that I had more in common with my sister than I thought.

Reading over the lyrics again, I knew the person who'd written them had plenty of reasons to be hopeful about the future—whether it came in the form of a sold-out show or a certain handyman who was quickly taking up all the real estate in her heart. Either way, she'd made it clear that she was about to have a hell of a ride ahead of her.

Chapter 7

In a nod to the old days, I stopped by Evelyn's house the next afternoon to play my new song for her. I couldn't wipe the smile off my face as I waited for her to answer the door. It was like going back in time, standing there with my guitar case propped up beside me, the tune of my song on a loop in my head while I imagined what her reaction would be.

When the door opened, my best friend was wearing a sympathetic smile. "Cassidy must be drowning you in *I told you sos*. First, she gets you to come back home, and now you're already writing music again."

"She hasn't said those exact words yet, but I know she's thinking them."

"If you decide to sing at the concert, she'll say it right to your face." Evelyn led the way into her house and made a right into her bedroom. At the threshold, she spread out her arms. "Behold, the room that hasn't changed since I was fourteen."

I laughed. "It suits you, then."

"Speak for yourself."

As I stepped into her room, the familiarity of it cocooned me in its warmth. Every detail matched the image that lived in my memory, from the tie-dye comforter to the dreamcatcher hanging on the wall beside her bed. Vinyl records and CDs were stacked high in almost every corner of the room, and her Hollywood-style vanity mirror still sat proudly in the center of her dresser.

I turned to Evelyn and smirked. "The only thing that's missing is the Jonas Brothers posters."

She laughed. "Hey, who says Joe Jonas still isn't the love of my life?" Grimacing at the décor, she said, "As soon as I can afford to buy my dream house, I'm going to design the perfect room. You'll see."

I walked over to her desk and picked up the old-school radio that had Evelyn's initials inscribed in glitter ink. "I cannot believe you still have all this stuff."

"I use it as motivation to start planning my escape. Living with my parents is suffocating."

"I'll remember to tell that to Jade, who's still convinced she has the worst parents in the world."

As I casually surveyed her room, she cleared her throat. "So, are you going to play me your masterpiece or what?"

I eyed my guitar case, a foreign wave of self-consciousness settling over me. I'd never been nervous to perform in front of anyone before. And definitely not my best friend since kindergarten.

Reading my mind, Evelyn threw me a disbelieving look. "Don't tell me you're nervous."

"A little," I admitted. "This is my first time playing in front of anyone in years."

"I'm the one you perform with every time you get up on stage. I hardly count as anyone."

I smiled, grateful for my friend's ability to dissolve my unease. I looked down at my guitar again and took a breath. When I was focused on my instrument, it was only about me and my music. Everything else faded into the background until it almost ceased to exist.

I began to play—slowly at first but settling into a rhythm as my confidence grew. After a brief intro, I launched into the lyrics to accompany the music. Soon enough, I was singing like I was the only one in the room. Like I'd never stopped using my voice in the first place.

When I strummed the final note, it seemed to echo through the small space. The sound of Evelyn's applause rang through the air. When I looked up at her, I saw that she was beaming. "Okay, I know I always say this, but that was seriously incredible. I mean, your old songs were great, too, but this was on a whole different level."

I couldn't ignore the way my spirits took flight. "Really?"

"Big time. I can tell you've had a lot of experience since your last album."

It might have been one of the biggest compliments on my music that she'd ever given me. I felt a genuine smile take over my face. "That means a lot. Really."

She rested her chin on the back of her desk chair and gave me an impish smile. "Of course, now it's time to guess who inspired these beautiful lyrics."

My heart tumbled as she forged ahead with her analysis. "So, the first couple of verses are obviously about your personal struggles. There's no questioning that. But in the third verse, you say, 'You gave me a reason to hope again.'" She raised her eyebrows. "Wanna shed some light on that, Taylor Swift?"

"I'll pass."

She shot me a look. "You didn't come all the way over here just to leave me hanging."

"You barely know him."

"So I at least *sort* of know him. That's good enough for me."

I took a moment to plan my words carefully. Whatever was blossoming between Dustin and me was still nebulous, and I hesitated to put a name to it. Sure, I couldn't get his kiss out of my mind, and I could still feel his arms around me while we danced. But referring to myself as his girlfriend felt wrong, like I'd accidentally put on someone else's name tag by mistake. Still, I wanted my best friend to know about the man who'd been starring in my fantasies for the past couple of weeks.

I sat cross-legged on her bed and faced her. "Do you remember Dustin Cooper from school?"

She thought for a moment. "The one from Alabama? Who was in our math class?"

"Georgia. And, yes."

She smiled as recognition crossed her face. "Oh, I remember him. He had a huge crush on you all through high school. He must be pinching himself now."

"It seems like the whole world noticed except me."

"Well, you weren't exactly looking for a guy back then. You were married to My Chemical Romance and Paramore, remember?"

I winced. "Unfortunately, I do. I honestly have no idea what he saw in me back then."

Her lips curved into a half smile. "What about you?"

"What do you mean?"

"Don't take this the wrong way, but he doesn't seem like the type of guy you'd normally go for. But maybe I'm completely off." Her smile broadened. "Maybe you've always dreamed of having a big, cuddly southern boy to keep you warm at night."

"You're even worse than my sister."

"The difference is she's serious." She looked at me expectantly. "You still haven't answered my question."

I paused, thinking back to the first day I saw him again. "Cassidy sent me on an errand at Cooper Hardware a couple weeks ago. Of course, she didn't actually need me to buy anything. She knew he would be there. And I guess, somehow, she knew that I wouldn't see him the same way I saw him in high school. The way he looked at me, and the way he made me feel right at home… I've never felt like that with anyone else. You're right that I wouldn't normally pay attention to someone like him. But that all changed in a few minutes."

Her expression softened at my words. "Wow. You're really into him. So, you two are dating now?"

"Well, not exactly dating. He hasn't taken me out on an actual date yet."

She raised an eyebrow. "But you gave him a coveted spot in your lyrics?"

"We talk, mostly. But we never really have a plan. We just kind of go where the wind takes us."

"Mysterious. And where has it taken you?"

"Well… He kissed me yesterday. And it was pretty amazing."

She smiled. "By that look on your face, I can tell."

"It still feels surreal. Like I'm going to wake up tomorrow morning and realize this was all part of a long, crazy dream I had."

Evelyn sank lower into her chair and groaned. "You know

what this means, right? I'm officially the only single woman in this town over the age of twenty-five. I was counting on you to keep me company in that category for at least a few more years."

"Whoa there. I never said we were in a relationship." I thought for a second. "Besides, isn't Lily Johnson single?"

"She doesn't count. I'm pretty sure she plans to join a convent soon." Evelyn crossed her legs. "Anyway, how's the summer concert lineup coming along?"

"Pretty good. I told Madison she'll be performing, and I'm going to see Jake Haywood tomorrow night. I have a feeling he'll be the next big name in country."

"Sooo, you only have one artist so far. And she can barely face a crowd."

"Once I work with her, she will."

Evelyn sighed. "I know you won't listen to me, but what you played for me just now was better than any of the songs Madison played at the show. And I'm sure people would agree if you performed this August."

"You really think that?"

"Do I ever lie when it comes to your music?" She stood from her chair. "By the way, if you play that song for Dustin, I bet he'll say the same thing."

My breath faltered as I pictured myself singing for Dustin and letting him into that corner of my life. I pictured his kind eyes and easy smile filling me with encouragement whenever I started to lose my footing. Then, I imagined that same face in the crowd as I debuted my song at the summer concert, lifting me up and giving me the courage I needed to make it through.

I shook my head to dispel the images. What was I thinking?

I needed to stop spending so much time with Cassidy.

Chapter 7

* * *

When I opened the front door, I heard Jade's voice coming from the living room. Except it wasn't her voice. It was a lighter, sweeter version of her usual sarcastic tone, as if someone had dipped brussels sprouts in honey. I listened for a moment, questioning if it was really Cassidy's daughter, when Jade rounded the corner and headed for the stairs. She offered up a radiant smile. "Hey, Aunt Bailey."

"Uh, hi." The words came out like I was chewing and speaking at the same time, but she didn't seem to notice.

Cassidy approached me with a question in her eyes. "Where's Jade, and can I have her back?"

"I was just going to ask you the same thing."

"She hasn't spoken to me like that since before she hit puberty. It must be a boy she met. This is the age, I guess."

The reason suddenly hit me as I flashed back to my conversation with my niece. "Or it was her cool aunt," I said, smiling.

"What did you do?"

"I had a little chat with her the other day. I told her to cut you some slack because you're doing the best you can. Oh, and I even mentioned the time Mom grounded me and took all my CDs away when I changed out of my dress at the eighth-grade dance. That definitely put things into perspective for her."

"Well, at least she found one adult she wants to listen to." Cassidy hugged me. "Thank you so much."

When we pulled away, she had an amused look on her face. "I completely forgot that Mom did that, by the way."

"I wish I could forget."

My phone dinged with a reminder for tomorrow night's concert. Remembering that Lauren had given me an extra ticket, I glanced at my sister. "Hey, wanna come to a Jake Haywood concert tomorrow? I'm thinking about adding him to the summer concert lineup, so you can think of this as a preview."

"You should tell Dustin you have an extra ticket."

I froze. "But that would be like a…"

"Like a date?" Her smile was almost jubilant. "Yes, Bailey. That's what people do."

I looked down at the floor, but I could still see her no-nonsense look. "Oh, don't act all shy now. So far, you've danced with him on the lawn for the whole street to see and gone full lip-lock in front of my six-year-old. I'd say a proper date is long overdue."

"But that's just it. Those moments were spontaneous. A planned date is different." I ran a hand through my hair, thinking. "Besides, he doesn't even like that kind of music. He once told me he only listens to old-school country, like Conway and Waylon. Country pop might as well be Justin Bieber to him."

"If you think he'll be there for the music, you're even more clueless than I thought."

I felt my face redden. "He's probably busy with the store, then."

Cassidy considered me for a moment. "I know exactly what's going through your head. It's starting to feel too real now, and you're not ready. But that's exactly why you need to ask him."

As usual, she'd unveiled my every thought. I sat on the couch in defeat, my body sagging under the weight of the reality I had no choice but to face. "You're right. I'm not ready at all. When we danced and kissed, I wasn't thinking about what was going to happen. I was just living in the moment, and it was an amazing feeling. But ever since I wrote my new song, I've been able to step back and really look at what's happening in my life. And that made me see how quickly things are moving."

"Hold on a second. Back up." She planted her hands on her hips. "You finished writing the song?"

I shrugged, trying to appear nonchalant. "It's nothing special. Just a little something I put together."

"Aren't you going to let me hear it?"

After thinking for a second, I decided there was something I would much rather do instead. And this was my chance to get away from my sister's prying eyes. "Let me just practice it one more time, okay?"

Before she could respond, I headed up the stairs and slipped into Eric and Cassidy's room. After rummaging through the top drawer of the bedside table, I extracted the small notebook where Cassidy had painstakingly recorded all her contacts in alphabetical order. I scanned the last names until I reached the Cs and rested my finger on Dustin's cell number. Beside it, Cassidy had written *Repairs*. My pulse kicked up a notch as an image of his strong, steady hands drilling a hole into the tree house flashed through my mind.

After punching in his number, I disappeared into my room and shut the door. I perched on the edge of my bed while I waited for him to answer. When he uttered a greeting into the other end, I straightened. Showtime.

In my best impression of Cassidy, I said, "I'm so sorry to bother you. One of the tree house boards is loose. Do you think you could come and take a look at it?"

"I'm sorry, ma'am. I thought I bolted them down pretty well. Mind if I swing by tomorrow?"

A giggle escaped me. "Gotcha."

"Bailey?" He chuckled. "You sure got me there. You sounded exactly like your sister."

"Years of practice."

"So, I'm guessing you didn't call about the tree house, then?"

"Not exactly. Unless you're dying to teach me about drill bits."

He laughed. "I'd be happy to, if you're up to it."

For a moment, we were both silent, and I relished not feeling the need to fill it up with empty words. The concert resurfaced in my mind after a beat, and I remembered that was the reason I'd called him in the first place. "So, my boss gave me two tickets to a Jake Haywood concert tomorrow night. He's this new country-pop artist. I know it's not the type of music you usually listen to, but I was thinking maybe we would have a good time. Together." My face burned. "I mean, if you're not up to it, I totally understand, but—"

"I'd love to come," he said, and I could hear the smile in his voice. "You don't even have to convince me."

My heart flooded with equal parts relief and apprehension. "That's great. I didn't know you were into that kind of music."

"I'm not. I'm into the girl who's taking me there."

Just like what Cassidy had said. She really was right about everything.

"So, is this for your job?" he asked. "You said your boss gave you the tickets."

"Yeah. Jake's a candidate for the summer concert. I just want to see how he is in front of a crowd before I book him a spot."

"You're still not performing, huh?"

"I wasn't planning to," I faltered.

There was a lengthy pause, and I wondered if one of us had lost the connection. After a minute, he said, "Do you know why the crowds at the summer concert kept getting bigger and bigger every year?"

I meditated on his question for a minute. "Well, I know Pauline and Seth at the arts center have a great email campaign. And once people started bringing their friends and relatives from out of town, word got around pretty fast."

"No. It was because of you, Bailey. People came to see you perform. Ever since you left, we've had less than half of the usual crowd. That's not a coincidence."

My mouth dried up. "But Cassidy told me that Annabelle was the one people cared about."

"Annabelle was great too. And it's a tragedy that she died so young. But she wasn't you. Anything she did well, she probably picked up from watching you own the stage."

Cassidy's warning from my first day in Oak Plains reappeared in my mind: *If you don't perform, we'll have to cancel the entire concert.* It had been so easy to shrug off her comment back then, to tell myself she was only exaggerating. But hearing the same words come out of Dustin's mouth somehow gave them more weight. Was everyone really depending on me the way he made it sound?

"You had something different. And people noticed. That's why they stopped showing up."

For some reason, his words made me think of my meeting with Madison again. "You know that other singer I booked for the concert? Madison Brenner?"

"I remember."

"She was there. At my last concert. And she told me she remembers this girl running off stage and never performing again. She didn't recognize that it was me, thank goodness. But I haven't been able to get it out of my head ever since."

Gently, he said, "There's probably a reason for that."

"I feel like I failed her. She told me she's still waiting for me to sing again so she can believe that redemption is possible." I swallowed thickly. "The past six years, I never even considered getting up on that stage again. But the longer I stay here, the harder it is to walk away like I did last time."

Opening up to him dislodged a heaviness in my chest that I never knew was there. I felt like I could trust him with anything, and that feeling filled me with warmth.

"Remember when I took you to your old house? You couldn't even look that way in the beginning. But as soon as you heard the music and started dancing, you forgot all about the bad memories." He paused to let the memory sink in. "That's what the concert will be like. Sure, it might be a little tough when you get on stage, but you'll forget all about the fire when you start singing. And then you'll have the time of your life."

My throat tightened as I imagined his prediction coming true. My soul longed to feel the freedom of singing my heart out onstage. It longed to feel the rush of peeking out from backstage to see hundreds of people gathered to hear my music. I even missed having Evelyn accompany my guitar playing. Whenever I needed a confidence boost or just a reminder of why I did what I did, she would always be beside me, the rock I didn't know I needed.

"You don't want to miss out on all the good parts 'cause you're too afraid to relive the bad parts. Give it a chance."

As I pondered his words, my gaze drifted to the guitar propped up on the wall opposite my bed. I smiled to myself. "Not that I'm going to perform, but if I did, I would probably sing the new song I wrote."

"I knew you had more music in you. Well, what are you waitin' for? You gotta let me hear it."

I gave a nervous laugh. "Right now? You're not serious, are you?"

"Do I sound like I'm joking? As my granddad used to say, there's no time like the present."

I stared at the instrument, as if it somehow held the answer to how I would get out of this situation. But I knew I couldn't spend the rest of my life running away. And Dustin, of all people, deserved to see me for who I really was. My true self. The person I was desperately trying to distance myself from but who needed her time to shine.

I picked up my guitar and rested it on my lap, my fingers gently probing the strings. "I've only played the song twice, so it might not be perfect."

"I don't want it to be perfect. I want it to be *you*."

There was a tenderness in his voice that made my heart stutter, and I silently cursed him for throwing me off right before I was supposed to sing. I took a deep breath and tried to center my thoughts. Like I had with Evelyn, I concentrated on my guitar so that nothing else interrupted my focus. Once I had the song resounding through my mind, I put my phone on speaker and began to play.

He didn't utter a word the whole time I played. After I hit the last note, he said, "That's what you've been holding back all this time? No wonder your sister called you all the way back here to perform."

I couldn't help but smile to myself. Hearing his words made me feel like the young musician I once was, brimming with enthusiasm and potential. He made me want to be that person again.

"I'm glad you liked it."

"Liked it? That was incredible. Wait 'til everyone else hears it next month."

I opened my mouth, about to remind him that I still hadn't decided if I wanted to perform, but then I closed it promptly. Ever since he'd brought up our visit to my old house, something else had been occupying space in my mind. Normally, I would've opted to keep it to myself. But singing in front of Dustin made me want to share my innermost thoughts with him.

"Can I ask you something?" I said.

"Anything."

"How do you know when you've moved on from the past?"

He was quiet for a minute as he weighed my words. When he finally replied, he spoke in a sure, measured tone. "When you spend more time thinking about where you're headed than where you've been."

His answer struck me—not because of its truth but because of the way he said it. It sounded like he was speaking from experience, from a private knowledge that only he held. As an intense longing to visit that place overcame me, I wondered if he would ever feel comfortable enough to take me there.

"Why do you ask?"

I drew in a breath. "Ever since you took me to my old house, I haven't been looking behind me as much. I'm just focused on where I am now. Being with you makes me want to live in the moment."

"The song spoke for itself, you know," he said teasingly. "Everything you just told me was written out in the lyrics." After a beat, he added, "Just so we're clear, though, you're not the only one who feels that way. And I'd love to see where this thing takes us, if you're up to it."

My heart broke out into a sprint. "That sounds like just the kind of thing I had in mind." I bit down on my lip. "See you tomorrow night, then?"

"I'll be there."

After we reluctantly exchanged goodbyes, I was downright giddy and had more energy than I knew what to do with. I shot a glance at my closed bedroom door and got up to lock it. Then, I connected my phone to my Bluetooth speaker and put my favorite playlist on full blast. I started to dance like there was no one else in the house, like my sister wasn't still waiting for me to play my song for her. I felt free. Freer than I'd felt in a long time.

I knew my genuine self had always been waiting somewhere inside me for permission to break free. Maybe I'd finally gathered the courage I needed to let her out of her self-inflicted prison and allow her to have a say for once.

Chapter 8

The contents of my closet were spread out across the floor the next day, covering almost every visible square inch. The last time I put this much effort into finding the right outfit was at my last concert. Somehow, though, Dustin's opinion of me mattered more than the collective opinion of an entire audience. I saw everything through his eyes, whether it was my clothing or the words I chose in front of him. I'd willingly put myself in the spotlight countless times, but sharing the cab of his truck with him for the next two hours was a much bigger, brighter spotlight. One that rendered me uncharacteristically self-conscious.

Before I could decide if the sundress was the right choice, Cassidy burst into the room. I turned and glared at her. "Knock much?"

She snorted. "You always forget that we used to share a room." Eyeing the sea of clothes by my feet, she said, "I don't remember calling the producers of *Say Yes to the Dress*."

"Normally, I'd pretend to laugh at that, but I'm too stressed to even try."

Cassidy sat down on the floor beside me and pushed a mound of clothes off to the side. "Why are you acting like this? You already know he's crazy about you. Hell, you could show up in tattered sweatpants and he still wouldn't be able to take his eyes off you."

I sighed. "I don't know. I guess I'm just nervous. I haven't been on a date in ages."

"I get it. But you're wasting your time by stressing out about what he thinks. Remember, he was still attracted to you when you went through that Hot Topic phase."

I buried my face in my hands in mock horror. "I still can't believe anyone let me go out in public with those shredded leggings."

"Don't forget the skull-and-crossbones belts."

"Just when I thought it couldn't get any worse."

She smiled. "All I'm saying is, don't try to fix what's already working. He likes you for you."

"I hope you're right."

"I am." She got to her feet and eyed my outfit again. "Now put on something you really want to wear."

"What's wrong with this?"

"It's not you." After shooting a glance at the pile of clothes on the floor, she unearthed a peasant top with loose, flowing sleeves. "This is you."

"That was me when I was twenty."

"You mean when you weren't afraid to be yourself?" She dangled the top in the air until I had no choice but to accept it.

"Fine. But I don't see what difference this is going to make."

I put on the top and walked over to the mirror above the dresser. The second I caught a glimpse of myself, I knew I was wrong. It made a world of a difference. Somewhere behind the past six years that had worn me down, I could see the free spirit I used to be. The girl who was always eager to seize life in its fullest, purest form. The one who was always inclined to follow her own path, no matter what that looked like to the people around her. The person who was, as Cassidy had rightfully pointed out, *me.*

"You're right," I said, turning to her. "It's perfect."

"You're welcome."

My phone lit up with a news alert, and the time caught my eye. "He's going to be here any minute."

"To come whisk you away on his white horse? Or, should I say, his dusty Chevy."

"Ha ha. I'll take the Chevy, thanks."

When the sound of tires crunching on gravel trickled through the open window, a dizzying mix of excitement and nerves seized my chest. I turned to Cassidy. "How do I look?"

"Like you're about to pass out."

I cut my eyes at her, and she laughed. "Don't worry. Your pale skin complements your outfit beautifully."

"We're done speaking."

The sound of her laugh followed me out into the hall as I fumbled my way downstairs. When the doorbell rang, my heart started knocking against my chest, forcing me to catch my breath. I sternly reminded myself that I'd once performed in front of over five thousand people at a benefit concert. Surely, the same person who'd effortlessly taken on that crowd couldn't have wobbly knees at the idea of attending a concert with a guy she'd known since eleventh grade.

I opened the door with what I hoped was my most relaxed smile. "Hey," I said, the slight tremble in my voice belying my calm front.

"Hey." His eyes rested on me for a moment. "You look great."

"At least someone thinks so." I turned around and glared at my sister, who was still watching me with a mocking smile from the foot of the stairs.

He chuckled softly. "I think it's in the sibling job description to give us a hard time whenever they have the chance. I know my sister would do the same thing."

How did he manage to make me feel so at ease about the smallest things? Despite the way my heart threatened to climb out of my chest, I felt a sense of security around him that I didn't feel with anyone else. It was an intuitive sense that I was appreciated for who I really was. I didn't have to hide. That simple fact stroked me like the gentle touch of a summer breeze.

As I climbed into the cab of his truck, I thought back to the first time we'd driven together. Somehow, it felt different this time. It seemed like we knew each other more intimately now even though we'd only spoken to each other a few times since then. I glanced at him out of the corner of my eye, wondering if he felt the same way.

We started off, making our way down local roads that snaked toward the highway. He cleared his throat. "There's usually a lot of traffic once you get into the city. Hopefully it's not too bad."

His usual smooth way of talking was absent, and I wondered if he was as nervous as I was. "I know what you mean," I said. "My office is only about twenty miles away from Ackerdale, but it takes at least an hour to get there during rush hour."

"Can't imagine how far it is from here."

"I'm lucky if I can get there in under three hours. That one time my boss called me in last week was pure torture."

He was silent for a moment as he focused on the road. "How long you plan on staying at your sister's house?"

"I'm not sure. Maybe until after the concert." I looked down at my hands. "I guess I thought I'd be back home by now, but…"

My voice trailed off as the unspoken reason I was still here hung in the air between us. "I mean, I'm just grateful that Cassidy has been so generous. She's always been a great sister." I turned to him. "What about you? You have a sister too, right?"

I thought I saw the light in his eyes dim. It was no more than a mere flicker, but that didn't negate its existence. It reminded me of the way he'd reacted when I asked him why he left Georgia. What was he hiding beneath the surface?

"Two sisters and a brother," he said. "Only my older sister still lives here though. My younger sister moved back to Georgia, and my brother lives in Minnesota now. My dad couldn't stand selling our homestead to someone else, so he rented it out for a few years before my sister moved back."

"A Southerner taking on the Minnesota cold?" I said, trying to lighten the mood. "Brave soul."

Dustin smiled. "He met his wife up there in college and never looked back. He swears you get used to the weather, but I don't think I ever could."

"I know you think the winters up here are bad, but try spending a week in Minnesota in January."

"I wouldn't last an hour."

I laughed. In the silence that followed, I noticed that he had the radio on low. It was quiet enough that I couldn't identify the song. With a teasing smile, I said, "I see you're getting into the Jake Haywood mood."

"No way. Two hours of that stuff is more than enough for me."

"It's always been my tradition to play the artist I'm seeing on my way to the concert. But I don't want to force you to listen to any more Jake Haywood than necessary."

"I appreciate that," he said, smiling. "I don't know how that guy can call himself country in good conscience. It's just pop with a southern accent."

"Tell that to all the dedicated fans who'll show up at his concert."

"They're not worth convincing. But after tonight, you'll hopefully see that inviting Jake to perform at the summer concert is a waste of time."

"Don't count on it."

He shook his head, but there was still a smile on his face. "You're never gonna back down, are ya?"

In response, I raised the volume on the radio, where Lynyrd Skynyrd was playing. I looked over at him. "Happy now?"

He grinned. "I am."

We let the song play as we headed down the interstate, the unrelenting heat of the July sun holding us in its steadfast grip. Even at five in the evening, the temperature still hadn't climbed down from its high of eighty-nine. It was the kind of weather that kept most of the Northeast locked indoors with the air conditioning on full blast. I always took advantage of the quiet and spent those sweltering afternoons reading under the shade of a tree or playing guitar on the back porch. Everyone thought I was crazy, but I found a unique kind of peace in the stillness of nature when no one was around to disturb it.

Dustin stole a glance at me. "You're reminiscing."

I gave him a small smile. "A little. Happy memories from

when I was a kid."

He was quiet as a thoughtful expression crossed his face. "You know, even when we were in high school, you always seemed so focused on whatever was going through your mind. Sometimes, I asked you what you were thinking about, and you said it was just the test you had next period. But with that level of concentration, I thought you were dreaming up a top-secret scheme or somethin'."

I tried not to betray the surprise I felt. I didn't recall that interaction ever happening. "You sure remember a lot from our high school days," I said.

He kept his hand steady on the wheel, his face softening in the streaks of light that filtered in from the windshield. Finally, he asked, "Do you remember what you said when I told you I was from Georgia?"

I shook my head.

"Your eyes lit up and you said, 'What is it like there?' That was when I knew you were different. Everyone else either didn't care or treated me like I moved here from Siberia. You weren't like that. I could tell you kept an open mind from the minute I met you."

"You never told me that," I said quietly.

"You made me feel like this town was my home even when I was eight hundred miles away from home. But I didn't tell you any of that. And I really wished I had before you left Oak Plains." He let out a sigh. "But that doesn't matter now. It's all in the past." His eyes shone when he looked at me, and I knew it wasn't just the sunlight reflecting in them.

We spent most of the remainder of the drive hopping from one radio station to the next, with the occasional comment sprinkled in here and there. Mostly, though, I enjoyed sitting in companionable silence with him and finding peace in living in the moment. It struck me how differently I used to behave before I met him, when I craved constant stimulation and always felt the urge to busy myself with something. In Dustin's company, simply existing alongside him was more than enough.

When the concert hall came into view, a thrilling thought planted itself into my mind. What would it be like to see a parking lot filled with people making a beeline to see me? It was a fantasy I hadn't entertained in years, and I wasn't sure why I chose to now. Maybe it was because the song I'd written was playing somewhere in the back of my mind, reminding me that I hadn't given up on singing just yet. I still hadn't forgotten how surreal it was to play in front of hundreds of fans who believed in my music as much as I did.

As we made our way into the lobby, my gaze landed on a gaggle of teen girls carrying vibrant posters plastered with Jake-adoring phrases. I smiled to myself as I recalled Evelyn spending hours crafting posters professing her undying love for the Jonas Brothers and then waving them enthusiastically at their sold-out shows. It made me long for a time when the possibility of being noticed by our favorite artist was enough to make our day.

We moved into a modestly sized theater, which didn't look like it held more than a few thousand people. After we settled into our seats, I turned to Dustin with a smile. "Ready for an hour and a half of pop with a southern accent?"

"Already tuning it out."

I giggled. "Don't worry. I don't think he has enough material to go longer than an hour fifteen."

"Let's hope."

After the opening act concluded, Jake's set began, much to

the delight of the elated fans surrounding us. Unlike Madison, the man appeared to have a natural command of the stage and his audience. He trotted around the stage like someone who started performing in the womb, and he interacted with his adoring spectators with the ease of someone hanging out with their closest friends. It was impossible to ignore the way the stage was like a second home to him.

His stage presence continued to absorb me as the show progressed. But there was something Madison had that Jake lacked, and it didn't hit me until the fourth or fifth song. Madison was a true musician. She had a pure love for her art that was almost palpable. It was clear that for Jake, performing was solely about showmanship. He failed to connect with the music in the way Madison did, a fact that only became more evident as he pounded out song after song.

Just when I thought he was going to wrap up the concert, Jake strode up to the microphone and flaunted his toothpaste-commercial-worthy smile. "I know some of y'all travel all over the country to see me play. And that means the world to me." His gaze roamed the crowd. "I know we've got some native Southerners out here. Raise your hands up high so I can see 'em."

Grinning, I grabbed Dustin's arm and raised it up for him. He promptly lowered it and said, "I'm not getting involved," but I still caught the mirth in his eyes.

"Well, I've got a special surprise for y'all," Jake went on. "I thought I'd go back to my Texas roots for this show and cover a song that's close to my heart. Here's Willie's 'Always on My Mind.'"

"Oh, hell no," Dustin said.

As Jake eased into the song, Dustin sent me an imploring look.

"Haven't I suffered enough?"

I bit down on my lip, trying to tamp down the fit of giggles that was about to break free. "Don't worry. I won't put you through any more torture."

I fought to keep a straight face as we made a beeline for the exit. The echo of Jake's soulless rendition of the Willie Nelson classic followed us out the door, sadly accompanied by the delighted screams of Jake's fans. Once we were outside the concert hall, peals of laughter tumbled out of me, making my limbs go weak. As I gasped for air, I said, "You should've seen your face. You looked like you were going to run down to the stage and rip the mic right out of his hand."

"I was closer than you think."

That only made me laugh harder, and Dustin started to laugh too. It felt like the easiest thing in the world, standing beside him under the pale-blue glow cast by the moon, sharing our joy with each other. I couldn't help but notice how we shared laughter just as easily as we shared silence. It made me want to ride all of life's moments with him—all the ups, downs, and in-betweens. There was no one else I imagined having by my side through it all but him.

On our way back to the truck, Dustin gave me a sidelong glance. "I hope we agree that you're not inviting him to perform at the concert."

"I was tempted to at first because he has such a loyal following. But he just doesn't measure up to the other artists who've performed at the show." I ran a hand through my hair. "I'm running out of time. So far I have Madison, this indie rock band called Slam that I discovered a few days ago, and Victoria Grant, a rising pop singer. If I don't find at least three more artists, then *I'm* going to have to fill one of the empty slots."

He leaned against his truck and regarded me thoughtfully. "Would that really be the worst thing?"

I bristled at the question. "Well, it wouldn't be ideal. It was never part of the plan to begin with."

He studied me for another moment before speaking. "You seem like you're pretty good at your job. You didn't get an A&R gig for nothin'. And your boss obviously thinks you're capable since she trusted you to put a great show together."

"What are you saying?"

"I'm saying, if you wanted to find someone who fits the bill, you would've done it already. I think the reason you keep putting off filling that empty slot is because *you* want to fill it. You keep saying you're going to find someone else, but let's face it. You would've made it happen already if you did."

I kicked a stray pebble on the ground. "You make me sound like some kind of diva."

"You're anything but that. All I'm saying is, the concert is in less than a month. You're gonna have to make a decision sooner or later."

I walked around to the passenger side and opened the door. "I choose later."

He didn't say anything as we traveled back down the headlight-studded highway, nightfall enveloping the cab of the truck. For several miles, we let the hum of the road fill the lull in our conversation. Words seemed superfluous, as if everything that needed to be said had already been said.

Once the vibrant city landscape had dimmed into hushed plains, a Wawa came into view. Dustin pulled into a parking spot. "You hungry? We can grab something to eat."

My stomach had been a bundle of nerves for most of the ride to the show, and I hadn't realized I was hungry until now. I smiled. "That would be great."

Inside the store, I scanned the shelves of snacks while Dustin browsed the ready-to-go meals. I was trying to choose between two different flavors of Sun Chips when I heard someone gasp.

I turned my head and saw a young redheaded girl staring up at me, her mouth frozen in a gape. She couldn't have been older than nine or ten. The girl tugged on another woman's arm and said, "Mom, that's Bailey Flynn!"

The girl's mother turned to face me and smiled apologetically. "I'm sorry to bother you. It's just that my daughter is a huge fan. She plays your music all the time."

My cheeks grew warm as the girl went on. "I have your album, *Wanderlust*. I've played it a million times. Whenever I listen to your songs, it feels like you're talking just to me."

I couldn't find words at first. I knew there were people out there who enjoyed listening to my music, but I'd always assumed they had some connection to my hometown. To think that my art had touched people I didn't even know made my throat tighten.

"That means a lot to me, sweetie," I said softly.

She stared up at me with big green eyes. "Are you going to make more music?"

Her innocent question was like a kick to the gut. I looked around me, as if to find the answer somewhere in the air, and saw that Dustin had been watching the whole exchange. He awaited my response with a sparkle in his eye, like he already knew what I was going to say. And in a single breath, I suddenly knew it too.

I smiled down at the girl, knowing I couldn't pierce a hole in her hope-drenched eyes. "You bet I will." Something else occurred to me then, and my smile widened. I looked up at her mother. "Where are y'all from?"

"Glenford. It's only a twenty-minute drive from here."

I turned back to her daughter. "Well, then it's your lucky day. I'll even be performing at the summer concert in Oak Plains this August. Do you know where that is?"

"Yes!" The girl practically started jumping up and down with excitement as she pulled on her mom's arm. "Will you please please let me go?"

"Of course, Emma." Her mother aimed a grateful smile my way. "Thank you. You just made this girl's day."

"No problem."

After they walked away, all the emotions swirling inside me stopped me from speaking. Dustin and I paid for our items and headed back to the truck while I tried to process what had just happened. Was I really going to sing in front of my hometown again? It was as if my mouth had made the decision before my brain did. As I settled into the passenger seat, though, I had a feeling I'd been leaning toward that choice this whole time. I just hadn't been ready to admit it to myself.

It was quiet after Dustin shut the driver's side door. Then, he threw his head back and laughed. "I can't believe a nine-year-old just backed you into a corner like that. There's no way you were going to say no to that sweet face."

I crossed my arms. "I'm capable of making my own decisions, thank you very much."

He wrapped an arm around me. "I'm just jokin'. But I owe that girl a favor for making you change your mind. Do you know how long I've been waiting for this to happen?"

I ran through the past ten minutes in my mind and felt a genuine smile spread across my face. It was then that I registered how excited I really was. I was going to sing again.

Chapter 8

It was really, truly happening.

"I need to start rehearsing my new song. And I should probably write another one while I'm at it." I was talking a mile a minute, but I didn't care. It had been far too long since I'd felt this excited about something. "I need to call Evelyn too. Hopefully, she's still up for playing guitar with me."

His eyes were awash with light as he pulled me close to him. "That's the Bailey I remember."

"Me too," I said, nestling my head on his shoulder. "Me too."

Chapter 9

I sat on the front porch two weeks later, strumming my guitar, my bare feet resting on the railing. I tilted my head back and let the soft whisper of a breeze weave its gentle fingers through my hair. The scene reminded me of summers that were still a series of vivid images in my memory. Summers where two full months off from school stretched before me like the vast backyard behind Cassidy's house. I could still taste the tangy lemonade that my mom used to pick up from the farm stand on Woodland Street. The memory was so crisp in my mind that it led me to wonder if they still sold the beverage there.

I rose from the porch chair and carried my guitar back up to my room. After slipping into the foyer to grab my keys, I jumped into the car and backed out of the driveway. I cruised down familiar neighboring streets before heading into the more rural part of town. As the roads widened and the landscape flattened, I spied the rows of tomato plants that belonged to the Cooke family. My mouth watered with the memory of the sweet juice that would explode in my mouth after a single bite of the fruit. We would add them to any meal we could while they were still in season—grilled cheese sandwiches, salads, and even my mom's fluffy scrambled eggs.

I parked below the Cooke Family Farm sign and walked into the barn, its doors splayed open to invite locals and visitors alike. When the cash register came into view, I was surprised to see Anna Cooke still poised behind the counter. Fred Cooke's daughter had been working at the farm stand ever since I was a young child.

"Hi, Anna." I smiled. "Good to see you again."

Her eyebrows disappeared behind her light-brown bangs as she looked up at me. "Bailey! I thought you were down in Pittsburgh? Then again, I've never really been tuned into the town news."

"Close. I live in Ackerdale, which is about twenty miles away from the city. But I'm staying at my sister's house while I prepare for the summer concert."

Her eyes lit up. "You're going to sing again? That's great! My family and I love going to the concert every summer, but it was never the same without you. Too much generic pop and wannabe hipsters."

"Well, it won't be like that this year. I already wrote a new song for the concert, and I'm in the middle of my second one." I felt a full smile warm my face. "I already talked to Evelyn, and she agreed to accompany me on the guitar. Just like old times."

"I'll hang up flyers in the barn here. Not that I'll need to. I'm sure word will spread like wildfire over the next few days."

I smiled gratefully. "So, what have you been up to?"

"Oh, nothing much. I'm working here all summer, watching over the store while my dad tends to his crops. I've got no complaints though. As my mom always said, idle minds are the devil's workshop. I figured I'd give him someone else to bother."

I glanced at the crops that wrapped around the field outside and the fresh fruits and vegetables lining the makeshift barn shelves, wondering if Anna found a sense of peace in following the same routine day in and day out. It was the kind of simple lifestyle I'd missed out on when I left Oak Plains, but I had a feeling I could get used to it.

"What about you?"

I jerked my head back to her, as if I'd forgotten she was standing there. The past six years funneled through my mind as I tried to extract a worthy fragment or two for my answer. But all I could think about was the way I'd done everything in my power to distance myself from my past instead of really living.

I offered up a casual shrug. "Just working. Lots to keep me busy in the music industry these days." I turned my eyes to the shelves beside her head. "Actually, I stopped by to ask if you still sell lemonade here. That used to be one of the highlights of my summer."

"Not this year, sadly. A whole swarm of beetles attacked our lemon trees earlier this month. My dad's usually good about keeping that from happening, but there's no telling when nature has other ideas."

"That's too bad." As I turned and scanned the store again, I noticed that a short line of customers had formed at the door. Facing Anna, I said, "I don't want to keep you any longer. Looks like you've got customers waiting."

She held up a finger to say "one minute" and walked out

from behind the counter. She plucked two cartons of fresh raspberries and strawberries from a nearby shelf and started bagging them. "Don't leave without these. Trust me, they don't get any sweeter than they are now."

I reached into my bag and pulled out my wallet. "How much are they?"

She waved off my question. "Don't worry about it. Think of this as a welcome-back gift."

I started to protest, but an older man at the front of the line cleared his throat with outward impatience. I thanked Anna before taking the bag and returning to my car. After unloading it in the back seat, I backed out of the gravel parking area and followed the road back to Cassidy's house.

The farm was only a vague mass of green in my rearview mirror when my phone rang. My stomach dipped when I saw Lauren's name, somehow sensing that she had bad news in store. "Hello?"

"What the hell do you think you're doing?"

Her cutting tone caught me off guard. Lauren had never been the touchy-feely type, but even her austere manner had a sheen of kindness over it. Until this point, she'd never overtly crossed the line into plain rudeness.

"I'm sorry?"

"I just visited the website for your big summer concert, and it says, in massive block letters, 'featuring Bailey Flynn.' Is this some kind of joke? You can't just boot out all the other talented artists and give yourself a spot."

The news took me by surprise. Although I'd confirmed to Pauline and Seth at the arts center that I would be performing, I hadn't expected them to feature me so prominently on the website. "I'm not booting everyone out. Madison, Victoria, and Slam are still performing. I just couldn't find anyone else promising enough to get up on that stage. And it's important to me that we continue my town's tradition of putting on a great show."

"So, you think you can do better than Jake Haywood? And what about that girl everyone keeps calling the next Maren Morris? This was supposed to be our chance at finding new talent. Not your own vanity project."

I tried to keep my voice level. "Actually, I've been performing at the summer concert since I was a teenager. I skipped the last few years because... Well, it's a long story. But everyone has been counting on me to get up on that stage again."

Her voice sounded guarded when she spoke, as if she was hiding the real reason my concert appearance upset her so much. "I've never even heard you sing before. I didn't know you sang, period. I expect you to blow everyone away, otherwise I'll have wasted my time trusting you with this event."

No pressure, I thought. As I pulled into the driveway, I wondered what seeing my name on the website had triggered in her. I understood being frustrated with the sudden change in plans, but this struck me as an overreaction.

"I'll leave you with this to think about," she continued. "Do you want to be practical and help other artists achieve their dreams, or do you want to take a one-in-a-million shot at hitting it big? Because when your dreams don't work out, it hurts to know you put your all into them."

I was still for a long moment as the line went dead. There was a distant time when I had aspired to hit it big. I would imagine my profile plastered on a bestselling CD, my lyrics being pumped out of car radio speakers across the country. But as I grew up, my dreams had become tamer, more practical.

Chapter 9

Working at a record company seemed like the best of both worlds. I was still spending my days surrounded by music, but my passion had a real-world application that allowed me to make a living.

Ever since I penned my first song in six years, though, I was suddenly bold enough to humor that sky-high fantasy again. Maybe I would never make a thank-you speech at the CMAs, but if my music could move one person like it did Emma, I had a feeling I would find the spring in my step that had long deserted me.

I finally opened the car door and mounted the porch steps, shopping bag in hand. When I stepped into the foyer, Eric was just slipping off his work shoes and shedding his blazer. He smiled at me in greeting. "Hot out there, isn't it?"

"Definitely the hottest it gets here." I raised the paper bag. "Hopefully these will cool everyone down. Fresh berries from the farm."

"Nice," he said as he peered inside the bag. "Leah's crazy about raspberries."

He placed the fruit on the counter and turned to me. "Word on the street is you're singing at the concert again. Cassidy was really happy to hear the news."

"I'm glad." I hesitated before adding, "Not everyone feels that way."

"What do you mean?"

I shifted my weight from one foot to the other, wondering how much I should share. "My boss found out I'm the main act now, and she... didn't take it well, to put it mildly. I understand that my decision was pretty last minute, but she wasn't just upset about the change in plans. It was almost like she was threatened by me performing."

A knowing expression crossed his face. "Doesn't surprise me at all. There are lots of people in the music industry like your boss. They worked hard to build a career making music, but they never made it. It's easy to become bitter when you see someone basking in even a fraction of the fame you wish you had."

I managed a small smile. "I don't think being well known in a town of three thousand people really counts as fame."

"Don't downplay your success. Plenty of people have noticed you, which is more than most aspiring singers can say."

Gratitude welled up inside me at his words. I could tell he meant every one of them. "Thanks, Eric."

"Did someone say raspberries?" Leah's feet came pattering down the stairs, and a smile teased my lips. The sound made me remember when I used to career into the foyer of my childhood home with the same level of enthusiasm.

My niece stuck her hand in the bag and helped herself to a handful of berries. Eric shot her a pointed look. "What do you say to your aunt for picking those out for you?"

"Thank you!" she exclaimed with a juice-stained grin.

"You're welcome, sweetie." I turned to Eric. "I'll see you guys at dinner. I'm just going to work on another song for the concert."

"Have fun," he said with a little wave.

I retired to my bedroom, where my guitar was waiting for me beside my dresser. I picked it up and sat with it for a moment, letting my mind run wild with whatever nugget of inspiration it chose to latch onto. For some reason, it landed on Anna, and I curiously followed the thread to see where it ended up. I closed my eyes and pictured the barn, the stretch of field outside, and the blossoming crops arranged in neat rows across the expanse

110

of green. Years ago, I would've dismissed that kind of life as one that belonged to a more simple-minded person. But after having stomached all the chaos and uncertainty of the past few years, taking a straighter, more tranquil road seemed like a breath of fresh air.

I began playing before the idea was fully formed in my mind. At first, my lyrics were more general, an out-of-focus picture of the simpler life I longed to live. But as I continued to play, I realized Dustin had found his way into my fantasy. In every image that flashed through my mind, he was there—sitting beside me on the porch on a pleasant summer day, wrapping his arms around my waist as we washed the dishes together, kissing me goodnight just before I drifted off to sleep.

I set down my instrument, feeling a frown crease my forehead. Did I really see Dustin as part of my future?

A flash of maroon above my desk caught my eye, and I rose to my feet. I walked over to the single bookshelf mounted on the wall and pulled out my high school yearbook, pleased to see that Cassidy had still held on to it. Flipping open to the senior portraits, I scanned the names until I singled him out among a sea of familiar faces. I studied our two yearbook photos, which sat only two rows apart. We were never far from one another, both on the page I was looking at and in the hallways of our high school. Yet for so long, he'd been nothing more than a figure passing through my field of vision, a mere face in the crowd.

Below each photo was a quote that each member of the senior class had chosen to sum up their four years. I still remembered the Oprah quote I'd plucked from one of my mom's old issues of her magazine: "The biggest adventure you can take is to live the life of your dreams." The uplifting tone made me yearn for the way I used to dream with abandon, nurturing my goals like a delicate plant.

I turned my attention to Dustin's photo again, wondering what he'd chosen as his quote. My stomach dipped as soon as I finished reading the Lynyrd Skynyrd lyrics about life's troubles coming and going like the ebb and flow of the tide. In the eyes of the calm, smiling boy above those heavy words, I glimpsed a veil of hidden pain. Those were the eyes of someone who carried a burden no one else knew about. I tried to think of where I'd seen them before and then remembered the times I'd gently prodded him about his past. He had always paused a second too long, spoken a little too low whenever he answered. And each of those replies were meager, ill-formed fragments of the bigger picture he neglected to show me.

With a heavy sigh, I closed the yearbook and placed it back on the shelf. Dustin had his own secrets, just like I had mine. If we were going to make this work between us, we had to let each other in, no matter how ugly the view was. Because the parts we kept hidden from view said more about who we really were than the parts we proudly put on display.

Chapter 10

"Are you sitting down?"

I looked up from my desk to see Cassidy standing in the doorway of the study. It was two weeks before the summer concert, and I was getting a head start on the work Lauren had assigned me that week. Now that I'd finalized my lineup and submitted it to the arts center, I found myself constantly worrying about whether I'd made the right choices. I not only had the success of the concert, but also Lauren's approval, riding on my shoulders.

"I assume you mean that in a figurative sense since I'm clearly sitting down."

She strode toward me, undeterred by my sarcasm. "You know how the summer concert always takes place in Alcott Park?"

"Every year, from what I remember."

"Well, not this year. The news about your appearance spread faster than we expected, so the arts center had to make some last-minute accommodations." She grinned. "So, it's official. We're moving the show to the Apex Center in Pittsburgh."

A jolt shot through my chest, and I couldn't decipher if it was one of anxiety, excitement, or both. "That arena holds, like, twenty thousand people."

"Yup. And they're all there for you. Well, the other artists, too, but mostly you. Before we announced your performance, we could barely fill up the park. This is going to be huge. Mom and Dad are even flying up here to see you. Isn't that exciting?"

"They are?" I'd seen my parents as sporadically as I'd seen my sister and nieces over the past six years. And considering the last time my mom and dad had seen me perform had ended in disaster, the sense of dread inside me far outweighed any excitement I felt.

"Yup. They called yesterday and wanted to share the news with you, but you were busy with work. They're just so happy you're going to sing again."

"But…" I started wringing my hands together, suddenly frantic. "What about the small-town charm of the summer concert? The whole point of it was to give people a feel for our town's musical talent. Why don't they just hold the Grammys there while they're at it?"

She studied me closely. "What's up with you? You haven't had stage fright since you were a kid."

"It's not stage fright. I'm just…" I let my face fall into my hands. "That's a hell of a lot of people counting on me to impress them. And now that it's been so long since I performed, the bar is higher than it ever was. What if I let everyone down?"

"By doing what? Being yourself? That could never happen. I know you have new material now, but as long as it's coming from you, everyone will love it."

Chapter 10

I tried to soak up her encouraging words, but I was too busy picturing staggered rows of seats filled with screaming fans, their eyes glued to the stage below. "Poor Madison. The girl's going to need a paper bag."

"She's still performing?"

I nodded. "I just couldn't bring myself to give up on her. I guess I just see a lot of potential in her."

"Good for you. I bet she needs someone like you to boost her up."

Something in my sister's words set off a light bulb inside me, and I leapt up from the desk chair. "Come to think of it, I bet she needs that right now."

Cassidy just looked confused, but I didn't have time to clarify. "I'll see you later," I called over my shoulder.

Once I was inside my car, I whipped out my phone and sent a quick text to Madison. A minute later, she told me she was already in Pittsburgh for a recording session and that she would meet me there. I tucked the phone into my bag and set off toward the city.

I arrived at my destination in record time, thanks to the off-peak hour. I paused after getting out of my car to drink in the sight of the arena towering above me. Unaccompanied by the pulsating energy of the crowd, the venue took on an eerily deserted feel. I tried to picture a full parking lot teeming with fans but failed to conjure up the image, despite how many concerts I'd attended over the past twenty-eight years. It all seemed more surreal when I was the one in the limelight.

As I strolled up to the arena, I caught sight of Madison standing by the main entrance, appearing deep in thought. I called out her name, and she started a little. Poor thing was already jittery, and the concert was two weeks away.

"This isn't a rehearsal, is it?" She asked the question like I'd arranged for her to dive headfirst into shark-infested waters.

"Not at all." I started for the door and tossed an encouraging smile over my shoulder. "Come on. You'll see."

There was still a note of hesitance in her eyes as she followed me inside. When the security guard tried to bar me from entering the backstage door, I showed him my ID and explained that I was one of the performers at the concert. After making a quick call, he nodded and ushered us inside.

The backstage area was a labyrinth of hallways and closed doors. I led Madison through the corridors until I stopped in front of a black door with faded white lettering that read *Stage Door*. I tugged on the handle, and the door pulled back like a curtain, revealing a cavernous space with rows of seats stacked like dominoes. Peering over at the stage, I glimpsed a long catwalk jutting out into the general-admission area. The view made me feel a bit lightheaded, as if my toes were curled over the edge of a cliff. But instead of shrinking away in trepidation, my entire body yearned to ride the wave of adrenaline that was lighting it up like firecrackers.

I turned around to see Madison still bolted to her spot by the door. "I think I'm gonna be sick."

I walked over to stand beside her. "You've performed in big venues before, haven't you? I saw you open for the Violet Hearts, and that was a much bigger crowd."

She lowered her eyes. "And you saw what happened then."

I considered her for a moment, then motioned for her to follow me over to the stage. I sat down on the platform, and she joined me, making a point to avoid looking up at the seats rising above us like stately columns.

"I used to have really bad stage fright when I first started

116

singing live," I said. "Just looking at the crowd made me freeze up and forget all the words. So I came up with a new strategy. Whenever I had a show coming up, I would go to the venue all by myself and sing up on stage in front of empty seats. It made me feel more in control, somehow. And it helped me get used to the view. That way, it didn't seem all that intimidating on the day of the concert."

Madison managed a small smile before glancing down at her shoes. "It's not really stage fright. Something happened when I was a kid, and I guess it still messes with my head now."

I waited for her to continue, and she did after drawing in a breath. "I had the lead role in my school musical in sixth grade. I spent hours rehearsing my lines and the lyrics to every song. On the day of the show, I was wearing a long, puffy gown. I was in the middle of my big number when I felt something scurrying under me. When I started to lift my dress, I saw a mouse right there in the middle of the stage. The scream that came out of me didn't even sound like it was mine. While I ran backstage, I heard Jenna and Lindsey—my worst enemies—laughing hysterically from the stage. They knew I was deathly afraid of mice and let one loose to mess up my performance. Which they successfully did." She let out a long sigh. "It's like the trauma of that day comes back to me every time I get up on stage."

As she told her story, it was as if there were an invisible thread joining us together. We'd both gone through traumatizing experiences that still stole our confidence at even the thought of performing live. Maybe the events that unfolded were different, but the feelings at the root of it all were the same.

I gave her a crooked smile. "Funny how we both had outside events cause our fear of performing."

Genuine shock mottled her face. "You mean you're afraid too?"

"I never used to be. But that changed six years ago. I was singing at the summer concert in Oak Plains, like I did every year, and then I heard all these sirens. My neighbor came up to me then and told me that my house had caught fire. By that point, though, it was already too late." I met her eyes with a meaningful look. "That was when I ran off the stage. Just like you remember."

Her mouth dropped open. "That was *you*?"

I nodded.

"Wow." Her large eyes were laden with sympathy. "I'm so sorry that happened to you."

"Thank you. But the important thing is that I got through it. And I don't want you to be held back by what happened to you either." I nudged her softly. "Just think about how much it'll bother Jenna and Lindsey to see you kick ass at the summer concert."

She smiled. "That almost makes it worth it."

I rose from my spot on the stage. "Well, then, let's see what you've got. I know I said this wasn't a rehearsal, but it helps to practice in a low-pressure environment."

Standing up slowly, she scanned the empty arena with wary eyes. "I haven't warmed up yet."

"Don't worry about how you sound. Just be yourself. Let go, and see how it feels."

It only lasted a second, but I watched her features harden into a look of pure determination. What I saw was only a mere spark in the fire that blazed inside her, torching any lingering traces of fear. I knew it because it was the same fire that had driven me to fill a slot in the concert lineup.

She opened her mouth and unleashed a feeble note that was swallowed up by the empty dome. Sending a worried glance my way, she said, "That was bad, wasn't it?"

"Nope. The quality of your voice is great. You just need to project more."

She gave a weak chuckle. "Guess that'll come in handy when I'm singing in front of twenty thousand people."

After a short pause, she cleared her throat and began again. This time, her voice carried all the way across the space, rippling from one end to the other.

I nodded in approval. "Much better. Just remember to work on your posture too. Act like you're Taylor Swift accepting her eleventh Grammy."

She stood up straighter and lifted her chin. "Like this?"

"Perfect."

I coached her through the entirety of the song, making sure every aspect of her performance was polished, from her moves to her voice. Her confidence seemed to rise with every run-through, even if it was only by a small degree. Regardless of her pace, I couldn't ignore how far she'd come since the first time I saw her sing.

I was in the middle of coaching her through her scales when my phone vibrated in my pocket. I pulled it out and felt my pulse quicken as Dustin's name illuminated the screen.

"I'll be right back," I called over to Madison. "Keep practicing."

I opened the stage door and slipped into a closet across the hall that was marked Storage. Lowering myself onto an overturned amp, I hit the accept button. "Hey," I said, my voice taking on an unusually husky quality.

"Are you home?"

"I'm at the Apex Center in Pittsburgh. Just doing an impromptu rehearsal with Madison. Why?"

"How quickly can you make it back home?"

"Well… I guess if I leave now, I can be there in a couple of hours. Is anything wrong?"

His voice was calm, in control. "Nothing's wrong. I just want to show you something. Something that means a lot to me."

I checked the time on my phone and saw that it was still early enough to beat evening rush hour. "I'll be there as soon as I can. Where is this place, exactly?"

"Just keep driving through town 'til you get to Deer Field Lane. You'll know it when you see it."

I made a mental note of the street name as we said our goodbyes. When I opened the stage door again, I saw that Madison was in the middle of one of her best solos yet. I felt guilty about leaving her hanging, but the mere thought of seeing Dustin again rendered me too distracted to coach her anyway.

"Hey. I'm going to head out now. I have, uh… an emergency meeting at work."

She stopped singing to raise her eyebrows at me. "On a Saturday afternoon?"

I faltered. "Well, the music industry can be really unpre-dictable. You always need to be on call." To distract her from my inadequate answer, I added, "You sound amazing, by the way. Keep up whatever you're doing."

She beamed. "Thanks. I'll try." For a moment, she thought-fully considered the seats that surrounded her. "I think I'll stay here a little longer. I want to make sure I have everything down pat."

"I'll be rooting for you," I said with a smile.

I started to go, but Madison's voice made me turn around again. "Oh, and Bailey?"

"Yeah?"

"Thanks for giving me a spot in the summer concert. For giving me a chance."

I smiled. "I can see your potential, Madison. And I know you just needed a nudge to unlock it. We all do, in a way."

Her expression was filled with gratitude as she waved good-bye and continued her rehearsal. I darted through the maze of hallways until I emerged into the parking lot. After unlocking my car, I slid behind the wheel and turned out of the lot. I couldn't shake Dustin's voice from my mind as I wondered what he wanted me to see so badly.

Once I'd entered Oak Plains, I turned onto Deer Field Lane per Dustin's instructions. I only ever drove down that street to make a U-turn, and I failed to call any of its specific features to mind. But as I tuned into my surroundings, I noted how the street set itself apart from the rest of Oak Plains. Houses were sparsely scattered on either side, most of them set back from the road. Imposing oak trees sprouted around each home, wrapping them in an embrace of thick, gnarled limbs. While there were oaks found all over town, I had the impression that the trees on Deer Field Lane had inspired Oak Plains' name.

I cruised down the quiet, shaded street, repeating Dustin's words in my mind: *You'll know it when you see it.* Besides the obvious beauty that adorned the view outside my window, nothing in particular stood out to me. I started to pull out my phone to call him when something caught my eye.

Stopping at the end of the street, I looked over to my left. The glistening water of a rolling creek winked at me, the unmistakable Chevy pickup staking its claim on the grassy bank. My heart soared at the sight of his truck. I jumped out of my car and shut the door before crossing the street to the creek.

As the body of water came into view, I spotted Dustin sitting on the bank, his body relaxed and his face serene. I went still as I watched him, wondering if the surface of the creek was reflecting his memories.

He must have sensed me as I approached him because he stood and smiled. "I knew you would find this place."

"The only reason I did is because I saw your truck. Before then, I couldn't figure out what you meant by 'you'll know it when you see it.'"

His eyes were bright as they locked with mine. "Look in front of you, Bailey."

I followed his gaze and felt the air leave my lungs. Looming over the edge of the creek was the majestic outline of the Appalachians. The mountains kept watch over the oaks, which looked stout in comparison. I felt myself disappear into the background as I beheld the sight in front of me, the towering gems now the stars of the show. Growing up on Acorn Lane, I noted that the Appalachians had always played hide-and-seek with the horizon, an elusive shape in the distance. To see them in full view almost felt forbidden, as if I were overstepping an unseen boundary.

"Wow," I breathed. My voice seemed to abandon me after I released that one syllable, as if it failed to form words for what lay in front of me.

Dustin's expression was full of mirth. "What did you think, I brought you all the way here to show you the Walmart parking lot?"

"I just didn't know this place existed. It doesn't seem real." I lowered myself onto the spot where he'd been sitting, my gaze still fixed on the mountains. I almost feared that by tearing it away, the staggering view would disappear right along with it.

Dustin sat down beside me and focused on the steady rhythm of the water. "I found this place when I first moved out here. I was missing my family and friends back home like crazy, and there was nothing I wanted more than to see some Georgia pines." A sad smile traced his lips. "So I started driving around, looking for an escape. This might not be the South, but it's pretty damn hard to beat this view."

"Looks like a close second to me." For the first time since I reached the bank, I noticed the fishing rod resting by his feet. "Doing some fishing?"

"Of course. This is the best spot for trout in the whole county." He looked over at me. "Ever gone fishin' before?"

"No, and I don't really plan to."

"Well, then I gotta teach you," he said, grinning.

I eyed the rod like it was radioactive. "I don't even know how to hold that thing."

He picked it up and stood next to me so that our shoulders were almost touching. "Like this."

A surge of electricity supercharged my veins at his touch. He indicated the different parts of the rod, and I followed along as best as I could without getting too distracted by the proximity of our bodies. After a moment, he adjusted the line with the aid of the reel. I watched his deft hands, which possessed the same certainty as they did when he worked with tools. I was entranced by his every movement.

When he was finished making adjustments, he guided my hand back to the rod. "Now pull your arm back."

I drew my arm back until the rod was vertical. "Like this?"

"Perfect. Now hold down this button here."

As I followed his directions, he helped me bring the rod

forward again, releasing the line and propelling the lure into the water.

I turned to him. "Now what?"

"Now we wait."

I snapped my fingers in exaggerated disappointment. "And just when I was getting into it."

Chuckling, he sat back down on the bank of the creek. I did the same while keeping my rod positioned properly.

He leaned back on his hands and shifted his gaze toward the horizon. I studied him out of the corner of my eye, my gaze sweeping across his beard and tracing his broad shoulders and chest. I wondered if I would ever grow tired of looking at him, if his features would become like the lyrics of a song I knew by heart. The kind I sang absently to myself while driving but without really focusing on the meaning.

He glanced over at me. "How'd the rehearsal go?"

"It went great. Madison's really starting to come into her own. I already see such a difference from the first time I saw her perform."

"Sounds like you're a great mentor to her."

"I'd like to think so." I turned to him. "How's business at the hardware store?"

His shoulders stiffened. "It hasn't been easy. My dad's been having health problems and can't do his job the way he used to. He blames it on working too hard, but we all know it's because of my sister."

It was only the second glimpse into his past that he'd allowed me so far, and I was loath to push his boundaries. Softly, I asked, "What happened with your sister?"

He didn't answer at first, and I wondered if he was afraid he'd already shared too much. After a weighted moment, he said,

"She got into drugs when she was a teenager. Got caught up in the wrong crowd in high school, and she was never really the same. She's been in and out of rehab for the past eight years. It's been rough on all of us, but my dad already had health problems before this all started. I'm constantly worried about both of them."

I reached over and touched his arm. "I'm so sorry. That's a heavy burden for anyone to carry."

"My mom always used to say that everyone has a cross to bear. If this is mine, I'm just trying to do the best I can."

I squeezed his hand. "I'm always here to talk, you know."

He gave a small smile. "I know."

He looked like he was about to share another fragment of his past that had long been tucked away. But before he had the chance to speak, I felt a tug on my fishing rod. I sat up straight. "I just felt something pull at me."

Dustin stood and gripped the rod. "This part here's important. You don't want to scare 'em away." As we held the rod, I felt the line jerk forward again. "Yep, that's a fish bite, all right."

"What do I do?"

"Same thing you did before." He showed me how to point the rod into the air like I did when I cast the line. "This is how you set the hook. Now we can start reeling in the fish."

I followed his lead as he started spinning the reel while raising the fishing rod. I watched in awe as a speckled fish emerged from the depths of the water, its scales iridescent in the late-afternoon sunlight. Dustin held up the rod with the trout dangling from the hook like he'd just secured the grand prize. He grinned at me. "Well, it's official. You caught your first rainbow trout."

"Now my life is complete."

He laughed. "Wait 'til you catch your first bass. Then you'll be transformed."

Lowering the rod, he gently deposited the fish back into the creek. "We're gonna let this little guy go. Let him reunite with his trout family."

I smiled as I watched the fish reenter the water. "You're a good teacher. I think I might even be able to do that myself next time."

"I try my best."

We stood there for a long moment, studying the calm water in silence. The air hung thickly around us as we met each other's gaze. Wordlessly, he cradled my face in his calloused hands and kissed me. It somehow felt deeper and more intense than the last two times, and I let my lips melt into his with a quiet desperation.

When we pulled away, I reached a finger to his face, tracing the contours that I'd come to know like the back of my hand. My fingertip thrummed with his heat while my heartbeat echoed an identical rhythm. I needed him all to myself, and the fire in his eyes spelled out the same desire.

"Can I take you back to my place?" he asked, his voice barely above a whisper.

"Okay," I said softly. Remembering that he lived alone, I was overcome with relief that I wouldn't be subjected to any prying eyes or questions like I would be at Cassidy's house.

My legs felt like they'd vaporized as they followed the path back to his truck. The all-encompassing quiet in the cab accentuated my every breath and heartbeat. By the time he turned onto Fern Street, I was convinced that every thought and feeling inside me was plastered onto my face, on full display for him to see as clearly as the street signs.

Chapter 10

He parked the truck outside his house and went still as the interior lights dimmed, painting shadows across his face. As I pressed my lips to his, he held me close, his fingers entangled in my hair. We stumbled out of the truck after a drunken moment and found our way up the front steps. After we entered the darkened house, we collapsed into each other, picking up where we left off in the truck.

We clung to each other as we found our way up the stairs, our breaths heavy in the stale air. It wasn't until he was lying in the same bed as me that the gravity of the moment dawned on me in all of its fullness.

While dusk cloaked the sky in a rich indigo, he loved me in a way I'd never been loved before. He made me feel uniquely cherished, as if I was the only woman he'd ever loved. Being with him was like coming home. A place where I felt safe, where my soul was laid bare. A place that I'd belonged to long before I knew it was mine.

As I fell back onto the bed with shuddering breaths, I closed my eyes and savored the aftershocks of the piece of time we'd carved out together. And, lying there with his breath still warm on my skin, I knew my heart had never felt as full as it did then.

Chapter 11

The next two weeks were bathed in the warm, golden light of the joy that had abandoned me for too long. Between my upcoming performance and my flourishing relationship with Dustin, it seemed that all the stars above me were aligned perfectly. I constantly caught myself singing—while washing the dishes, doing laundry, or even running errands. I was flying high, and I didn't ever want to come down.

The day after my night with Dustin, Cassidy had come out to the backyard where I was pretending to garden but was really lost in another daydream about him. She crossed her arms. "Those flowers aren't going to water themselves, you know."

I snapped out of my reverie and returned my attention to the dahlias, which were now in full bloom and radiating a brilliant pink throughout the flower bed. "I was just about to do that. Just got a little distracted."

She rolled her eyes. "Gee, I wonder why."

Before I could respond, she walked over and kneeled beside me. "I'm just teasing. I'm beyond happy for you. I really am. It's so nice to have the old Bailey back. And just knowing that you found someone who cares about you and wants you to be happy…" Her eyes glittered. "That's all anyone could really ask for."

I pulled her into a hug before she could see the unshed tears behind my eyelashes. "Thanks, Cass."

After stepping back, she paused for a moment, her gaze lingering on me. She seemed to take in the botanical bounty that sprang up in front of us, with me right at the heart of it all. A small smile crossed her face. "You look just like you did in that field of flowers on your album cover."

I thought about when Madison had seen the album cover in my office, and how she couldn't quite believe it was me in the photo. There was no doubt I'd strayed from the carefree girl I'd been on that cover. But now I could feel my muscles loosening into that person again. Maybe it was her time to shine, just as long as I let her have the spotlight.

In the couple of weeks that followed, my feelings for Dustin deepened along with my love for music. I penned songs faster than my mind could keep up with them, and I played them all for Dustin, who watched me sing like I was an angel watching over him. I ran through every lyric and note until it was etched into my mind like I'd written it out in permanent marker. Dustin was there through it all like a song I couldn't get out of my head. His smile was sunlight weaving through the trees, the twinkle in his eyes the sprinkle of stars in the sky. Whenever I saw him, it was like invisible Christmas lights illuminated me from within. Even Cassidy swore she'd never seen me like this with any other man. I'd only had two short-lived relationships before—one at the start of college and one in the time I'd lived in Ackerdale. But both of those relationships were nothing more than a faint glimmer compared to the blaze that Dustin had ignited in me.

A week before the concert on Saturday, my parents arrived in Oak Plains and made themselves comfortable in Cassidy's house, where they would be staying until Sunday morning. They had the chance to meet Dustin when the four of us went out to dinner one night. I'd been anxiously pushing around my food with my fork at the start of the meal, but I slowly relaxed once I saw how well they were all getting along. After we left, my mom took me aside and, with a gleam in her eye, said, "Someone like him doesn't come around every day. I can see how happy he makes you and how well he treats you. Don't let him go."

I knew every word she said had come from the heart. It filled me with joy to know that the way he made me feel was palpable, radiating from my whole body for everyone to see. It told me that this was more real than anything I'd had before.

In the past, I would've approached such bliss with caution, afraid of the inevitable fall that would ensue. I would never dwell on the fact that I was happy, as if being aware of its presence made it a tangible thing that could escape my grasp. Now, though, I let myself bathe freely in the feeling like someone who had an endless supply of it. Instead of seeing happiness as a finite resource, I felt secure in the knowledge that I would always have enough of it.

I still remembered when I'd asked Dustin on the phone how a person knew they'd moved on from the past. His response was just as clear in my mind: *When you spend more time thinking about where you're headed than where you've been.* For once, I could confidently say the past was in my rearview mirror, and I was letting the road ahead carry me to an unseen destination. But instead of worrying about where it would take me, I followed along with the open curiosity of a small child wandering through a new place.

The night before the summer concert, I lay beside Dustin in his bed, running my fingers across his chest. The crickets sang a song outside his bedroom window, as if they were the opening act before my performance. For a long time, we lay there without saying a word, soaking up the serenity of the moment we were sharing. I was making a concentrated effort to keep my anxieties at bay until the show began. The night was too pure to sully it with worries of how my debut performance would go.

I turned to him with a lazy smile. "You better come backstage with me tomorrow. I need a good luck charm."

"Course I'll be there. Even if I have to tackle the security guard."

I giggled. "I would pay to see that."

He pushed a stray hair out of my eye with his thumb. "You know you're the best thing that's ever happened to me, right?" he whispered.

His words struck a chord somewhere deep inside me, and my eyes moistened with tears. Alarm seized his face. "What's wrong?"

I smiled through my tears. "I just never thought I'd be this happy again. It doesn't seem real."

He pulled me close to him and rubbed my back. "It's real, baby. It's real."

As I breathed him in, I knew every word of what he said was true. And I let myself sink into the truth of his words as the beginnings of sleep caressed me.

* * *

The walls of my dressing room throbbed with the energy of the growing crowd. My hand shook as I applied mascara, creating a black smear just below my eyebrow. I cursed under my breath as I drenched a cotton ball in makeup remover and swiped at the smudge. At this rate, I would be barefaced by the time the stage manager issued the five-minute warning.

Evelyn swooped into the room with a stack of clothes draped over her arm. "I stole these from the dressing room down the hall. I have no idea who they belonged to, but they're yours now."

I whirled around. "Ev, you didn't have to do that. I already have an outfit picked out."

"Exactly. You have *an* outfit picked out. But this right here is *the* outfit, period."

I threw up my hands in surrender. "Fine. Show me what you've got."

She dumped the clothes onto a chair beside the dressing table and held up each piece. "This made me think of you right away," she said, displaying a fringed denim jacket with rhinestone-lined pockets. "And these pants will look great with these heels."

I took in every part of the outfit, which undoubtedly screamed me. But there was something amiss. Before I could put my finger on it, a flash of crimson caught my eye. I pointed to the piece of fabric. "What's that?"

Evelyn pried it free from the pile of clothing. "Just a dress I found. But I'm not sure it's you."

After pulling the dress over my head, I admired myself in

the mirror, twirling a little to show off the ruffles. Evelyn was right—it wasn't something I'd normally wear. But the woman who was about to take on a whole arena of fans didn't shy away from taking risks. Instead, she approached it with open arms, eager to see which direction she ended up taking.

"I have to admit, that looks amazing on you," Evelyn said.

I turned to her, beaming. It felt good to forget about my nerves for a moment. "I think so too."

There was a knock at the door. "It's me," Cassidy called.

Evelyn opened the door, and my sister stopped just outside the threshold. "Whoa. Dustin won't be able to walk in a straight line after he sees you in that."

"Is it too much?"

"Not really. You're just not used to making a statement. But if there's a time to make a statement, this is it."

I studied my figure in the mirror, feeling a fresh current of anxiety ripple through me. "I'm a nervous wreck."

"With that makeup job, I can tell." Cassidy crossed the room and grabbed my makeup bag. While she refreshed my face, she gave me a quick pep talk. "You've done this a million times. Sure, maybe the venue wasn't this big, but the size of the audience has never stopped you. Don't even think about the six years between now and your last performance. Just act like you're getting up on stage after a show you did the other day."

I sighed. "There's so much pressure on me now. It's hard to ignore how long it's been since my last show when everyone is making such a big deal out of me singing again."

She set down the blush brush and looked right at me. "It's impossible to let them down, Bailey. Unless you woke up this morning and sounded like Chad Kroeger, you have nothing to worry about."

In spite of myself, I smiled and told myself she was right. The packed arena that waited somewhere beyond the backstage door was proof of that.

As Cassidy finished up her makeup job, I craned my neck toward the hallway. "Where are all the other performers?"

"They're still getting ready," Evelyn said. "Weirdly enough, Madison doesn't seem nervous at all. I don't know what kind of magic you used on her, but the girl seems ready to seize the day."

"Figures. I'm the one sweating bullets and she decides to be the confident one now."

"Well, you must've given her good advice. Maybe you should try taking it."

I stared at my glammed-up reflection in the mirror and stood. "I'm gonna head to the ladies' room."

"This is your fourth bathroom break in like, an hour."

I turned and glared at my sister. "Didn't need the reminder."

After finishing up in the restroom, I paused in the hallway, taking a moment to collect myself. Out of the corner of my eye, I glimpsed a husky figure emerging into the corridor. As soon as he saw me, he picked me up and twirled me around. I started to laugh, unable to contain my giddiness. "You made it back here?"

"Yup. No security guard tackling needed." He paused and took me in for the first time. "You look beautiful."

I smiled at him. "I still can't believe I'm really doing this."

"You'll do great. I know it." He kissed me right there in the fluorescent-lit hallway, somehow making a spontaneous moment feel just as special and intimate as all the private moments we'd shared.

"Get a room."

I didn't even have to look up to see the grimace on Evelyn's face.

"They can't even hear you," Cassidy said. "They need a map to find their way out of each other's eyes."

"I'm going to pretend you didn't just say that."

I smiled against Dustin's lips. "Don't worry, Ev. There's someone out there who's perfect for you too."

"Tell that to my parents. They gave up hope for me a long time ago."

An eruption of cheers spilled out into the hallway. I shot Evelyn a panicked look. "Is that the end of Victoria's set?"

"Sounds like it."

Nerves flurried in my stomach. "That means Madison's on next. And then me."

Dustin's voice was gentle. "Just remember, you've been doing this your whole life. And everyone is here because they love you just the way you are."

As I hugged him gratefully, Cassidy scoffed. "Of course when he says it, you listen."

I heard someone approaching and turned to see Madison flaunting a black sequin top, leather pants, and black knee-high boots. Her freshly highlighted hair caught in the light, forming a sort of halo around her. She was almost unrecognizable from the mousy girl I'd met just a month ago.

"Wow. You look ready to get right on that stage."

Evelyn gave me a pointed look. "Unlike your mentor, who suddenly has stage fright."

"I feel great." Madison grinned. "That mini rehearsal really helped me feel more comfortable here."

"I'm glad to hear that. And remember, don't overthink your performance. You'll do your best if you just have fun and remember why you love singing in the first place."

"I know. Thanks to you." She beamed at me before turning and disappearing behind the stage door.

"Well, I'd better do some last-minute guitar exercises." Before she turned to go, Evelyn gave me a nostalgic smile. "Crazy to think we're back at it again after all these years, huh?"

"It is. But at the same time, it's like we never really stopped."

"I know what you mean." A wistful look rested on her face for a moment. "I'll see you out there. Break a leg, rock star."

"You too."

She clomped off in her cowboy boots as the opening of Madison's single that I felt sure would become a hit permeated the arena. It was strange to hear the notes she'd once played so feebly now being amplified in front of thousands of fans. They took on a new kind of power, an effect I knew well from the countless live shows I'd attended. I felt the music vibrate all the way down to my toes as I imagined my own song coming to life through the speakers—the one I'd modestly penned in my bedroom just a few weeks ago.

I turned and looked at the man who had reminded me that there was still plenty of life left inside of me. Who'd never left my side as I walked freely into that life with the unadulterated hope of a young child. As I soaked in the light inside his eyes, I felt tears tease my own. "I don't want this night to end. Ever."

"You've been waiting so long for this. You deserve every second of it."

I was cocooned in the inviting warmth of his arms when the stage manager's voice billowed out around us. "Flynn. You're on in five."

My heart began drumming out an erratic beat, and I pulled myself away from Dustin to steady myself. "So." I swallowed thickly. "I guess this is it."

"I'll be right here, rooting for you." He gave me one last kiss before letting me go. "Now show everyone what you're made of."

I walked over to the curtain, where the roar of the crowd was a wall of energy pressing against my chest. I closed my eyes, taking deep, measured breaths, until I heard my drummer start pounding out his solo. I'd told him to start getting the crowd pumped before I entered. Now, each strike of the drumstick went straight to my heart, creating a ballad of adrenaline that pulsed through my veins.

I drew in one final breath and stepped out onto the stage, where the spotlights doused me in their hot, blinding glow. The fans that I'd left in the dust for six soundless years greeted me with a deafening, collective scream of appreciation, echoing my relief to be back in the limelight. As I stood under the warm lights, feeling every cell in my body flicker to life, I knew this moment had been well worth the wait.

I strode up to the mic and flashed a smile at Evelyn. Seeing her there, guitar strapped across her chest, made me feel as though nothing had truly changed. I felt like I could simply open my mouth in front of all these people and they would be just as excited as they were all those years ago.

Evelyn jumped right into the song's intro, and I began singing the opening lines of "Different This Time." To my own ears, my voice sounded distant, and I felt as stiff as the high heels I'd paired with my showstopping dress. I hurried into the second line to smooth out the first, but I knew I didn't sound like myself. There was a certain quality absent from my voice. Something that made me sound like Bailey—and not Madison or Victoria.

I eyed my sky-high heels and frowned. How was anyone

supposed to feel like themselves in these skyscrapers?

"Y'all, I can't sing in these," I said into the microphone. With that, I kicked off the stilettos and discarded them off to the side of the stage. Sprinkles of laughter scattered throughout the audience, along with several cries of "Amen, sister!" I felt free, I felt whole, and best of all, I felt like me.

I started dancing barefoot onstage like I was in my own bedroom. For the first time since I stepped into the spotlight, I let myself have fun. It all seemed so insignificant all of a sudden—the concern for what other people thought, the need to win their approval. After all, the reason I started singing in the first place was because it allowed me to be the truest version of myself. As long as I was honoring my unique voice, it didn't matter how others responded to it.

The crowd seemed to be feeding off my energy. Even Evelyn played with a new sense of enthusiasm. It was like I'd picked up right where I left off that summer, as seamlessly as if I'd taken a ten-minute break. As I stood there giving my all, I couldn't help but wonder why I'd ever stopped.

The first song came to a close, and the spotlight crept up the stands, painting rows of spectators in expressions of pure, open-mouthed joy. I stood there for a moment, lapping up the feeling, the sight of thousands of people gathered here to see me. It was a humbling yet electrifying feeling to be a single person at the heart of such a staggering view.

I played a couple other songs I'd written for the show, including the piece inspired by Anna and her farm. When the final number of my set came around, I felt the mood shift around me, even though the change was imperceptible to everyone but me. I turned around and spied Dustin waiting in the wings, giving me an encouraging nod. I smiled and returned my attention to the audience.

"This last song is really personal to me. I wrote it when I learned an important lesson, which is to stop using the past as an excuse to avoid living the life you want. I spent years wallowing in my mistakes and regrets, and that kept me from living my actual life. It was hard as hell to admit that to myself. When I finally found the courage to let them go for good, I was able to see all the wonderful things that were sitting right in front of my face.

"This song is for anyone who's let the past stop them from living in the present. And, let's be honest, everyone in this room has probably felt that way at some point." I strummed the first note on my guitar and said, "This one's called 'All This Time.'"

Evelyn stepped back into the shadows, leaving the center of the stage to me and my guitar. It was an ode to the magic that transpired when I was alone with my instrument, creating the music that mattered to me in its rawest form. I sang as if it were still the week before the show, the arena still empty and swallowing up the sounds of my voice whole. Once I was deep into the song, I didn't even have to pretend anymore. I was one with the melody I created, the music as much a part of me as I was a part of it.

In the roar that followed my final note, I pressed my face into my hands, feeling warm tears tumble down my eyelashes. Evelyn ran over and hugged me tight as an indistinct sound from the audience grew louder. It took me a minute to realize they were chanting my name.

When I opened my moistened eyes, the crowd was a wet blur, but that didn't take away from the beauty of the moment. I found my way to the mic, where I managed to sputter out a warbled "Thank you." There was so much left to say, an infinite number of ways to express my gratitude for having this opportunity again. But as I took a generous sip of the view one last time, I knew an experience this rich was destined to get lost in translation.

Evelyn followed me backstage, a huge smile lighting up her face. "You were brilliant out there. Even better than I remember."

"You think so?"

"Of course. Didn't you see how the crowd was going crazy for you?"

A breathless laugh floated out of me. "I can't believe I just did that. That was... exhilarating."

Cassidy came careening over to me. "What on earth *was* that? If I knew you were going to be that amazing, I would've begged you to perform ages ago." She pulled me into a tight hug. "I'm so proud of you. I always knew you could do it."

"You were right. I never should've doubted you."

She gave my shoulder a squeeze. "All that matters is you came around eventually."

My mom and dad were the next to congratulate me. When I saw their faces again, my throat tightened until I couldn't squeeze a word out. I caught my mom's eyes filling with tears just before she wrapped me into a hug. "It's so nice to hear your voice again, Bailey," she said, her voice trembling ever so slightly. "You have no idea how long we've been waiting for you to do what makes you happy again."

The tears I'd been keeping at bay spilled out all at once. "Really?" I sputtered. "But what about—"

"Bailey, that summer is over. It's been over for a long time now," my dad said in his firm but gentle manner. He rested his hand on my shoulder. "What you just did tonight is what we've been waiting for you to do for years. You finally let go of this weight you've been carrying around, this guilt you don't deserve. And you were finally the Bailey we all know again."

I buried my tear-streaked face in his shoulder. I hadn't realized how much I needed to hear those words until he spoke them aloud. "Thanks, Dad."

I was wiping away my tears when Leah and Jade rounded the corner, followed by Madison. "You killed it out there," Madison said, grinning. "I can't believe you're the same girl who ran off the stage all those years ago. You've definitely found yourself."

"I can say the same exact thing about you," I said with a smile. "You were amazing."

She was quiet for a second, a reflective look on her face. "You know, I think I have you to thank for that. Remember when I said that ever since I saw that girl run off, I was waiting for her to redeem herself? Well, it looks like she just did."

My heart swelled with pride. "You're right. I really did."

After Madison left, the crowd that had gathered backstage started to thin out. The concert was over, and the screams from the audience had been replaced with an eerie silence. I'd been so swarmed with praise at the end of my set that I hadn't had a chance to look for Dustin. Why hadn't he been there when I returned backstage? I'd seen him standing just behind the curtain throughout my performance, but now he was nowhere to be found.

I stepped out into the hallway and scoured the narrow space for him. I peered into every room I passed and called his name, the sound bouncing off the thick cement walls. There was no sign of him, as if I'd dreamt that he'd come here at all.

When Cassidy rounded the corner, I rushed over to her. "Have you seen Dustin?"

She pursed her lips. "He stepped out in the middle of your last song. He said he had to take an important call." Glancing behind her, she said, "I think he's still outside."

I followed the maze of doors to the one that led outside, my insides coiling in fear. I told myself there was nothing to be afraid of, that I was just having déjà vu from my last concert. But my attempts at consoling myself were cold to the touch.

I was nearing the exit when the door opened. As his eyes met mine, Dustin pulled me into his arms—but it wasn't his usual bear hug. There was something lacking, something that had abandoned him along with the light in his eyes.

"You were great up there," he said as he held me. His voice sounded tired, as if days without sleep had finally caught up to him. "Really, Bailey. That was better than anything I've ever seen from you."

I ignored the compliment and pulled away from him. "Why did you leave halfway through the last song? And who were you talking to on the phone?"

His mouth formed a thin line. "That was my dad. Something just came up. I have to go back home."

"Oh." I tried to ignore the sinking feeling in the pit of my stomach and forced a smile. "I'll see you tomorrow, then?"

He shifted his gaze downward but not before I saw a sheen of moisture coat his eyes. "I have to go back to Georgia."

The blood in my veins turned to ice. I tried to breathe, but it was like my lungs had closed up. In a small voice, I repeated, "Georgia?"

The sadness that sank into his features made me want to pull him close, but the confusion and hurt I was feeling made me keep my distance. "I'm sorry, Bailey. But this is serious. Everyone needs me there."

142

"Who's everyone? Can't you just tell me what's going on?" I searched his eyes, desperation rising inside me. "I thought we had something real going on here. We can't keep things from each other if we want this relationship to work. What are you hiding from me?" My voice cracked under the pressure of my chest breaking open.

He grasped both my arms and looked me in the eye. "I need you to understand this, Bailey. You know me, but you don't know my family. Maybe one day I'll be ready to let you into that part of my life, but not tonight. Not when you looked happier than I've ever seen you. I can't take that away from you."

The realization crashed into me at full force. All the times I'd asked him about the ones he loved or the place he came from, he'd never responded with the openness I longed for. *You don't know my family.* Was he ashamed of them? Afraid that my feelings for him would change if I found out who they really were?

"I want to keep this picture of you in my mind when I leave. I want to remember you having the time of your life onstage." He swallowed. "That's the only thing that'll get me through this."

I stared at him blankly, trying to make sense of what was unfurling before me. I refused to believe that any of it was real. I wanted to see his big, easy smile take over his face as he assured me it was all a joke. I wanted him to lift me up like he'd done before my performance, his strong arms anchoring me to him. Instead, I was met with a deep sorrow etched into the crevices of his face that made him look much older than he was.

He kissed me, but it was rushed, so quick it almost didn't happen. "Please don't worry. I'll call you once things are sorted out. I promise." He started for the door, and only then did I see the panic in his eyes. Something bad had happened. Something very bad—and I had no idea what it was.

He was gone before I could say the words that had been sitting on my tongue the whole time. *But I do want to know about your family. I want to know everything about you. I would never stop caring about you or think less of you, no matter what you tell me. Don't you know that? I just want* you, *exactly the way you are.*

It was everything I should have said. If I'd spoken up, he might have told me what was going on—and I wouldn't be standing here wondering when I would see him again. But it was too late. The *should have*s always showed up after the damage had already been done. They befriended me once they'd proven themselves useless, just like they'd done after the fire.

I burst back into the venue, a single thought flashing through my mind: I'd never asked him how long he would be gone. Not that he'd given me the chance. He'd left just as suddenly as the cheers died down after the music stopped. So suddenly that the full gravity of his absence hadn't settled on my shoulders yet.

I didn't stop until I was in my dressing room. I started collecting all my things mechanically, as if I were connected to strings that were being manipulated by an unseen puppeteer. Last time, I'd waited until the next morning before packing a bag and setting off for Ackerdale. But I knew better now. The faster I got out of town, the less it would hurt.

Footsteps that I immediately identified as my sister's snuck up behind me. "You're leaving already? What about the meet and greet?"

"I have to stop by your house and get my things," I said flatly. "I'm going back to Ackerdale."

A pause. "You could've at least told me you were planning on leaving. And what about Mom and Dad? Aren't you going to say goodbye to them?"

"I will before I leave first thing tomorrow. They have an early flight, so we'll see each other in the morning." I started for the door, trying to ward off any other questions she might try to fling at me.

Cassidy stuck out her arm to bar my exit. "You're not leaving until you tell me what's going on."

My voice wobbled when I spoke. "He's going back home. To Georgia."

I caught the flash of shock on her face before she swiftly composed herself. "Do you know why?"

"All he said was that something happened at home with his family. I can tell it's serious. But he wouldn't give me any details. He almost seemed afraid to, like he thought I would change my mind about him if he said too much." I sighed, suddenly as exhausted as Dustin looked. "I think I just need to be alone right now."

I tried to slip past Cassidy again, but she blocked the doorway. "Maybe he just needs time," she reasoned. "He might be in shock from whatever happened. Once he's ready, I'm sure he'll tell you everything."

"How do you know he'll ever be ready?" I gritted my teeth, keeping a sob trapped in the back of my throat. "He's always been so secretive with me, almost like he doesn't trust me. And now I realize I should've said something a long time ago. I should've told him how much he means to me and how I accept him for who he really is. Then maybe he wouldn't be so afraid to show me all of him."

She steadied her gaze on me. "Please don't blame yourself for this too. The guilt will eat away at you, just like it did after the fire."

"You knew it, Cass. You knew how hard it was for me to let

someone in. But you still sent me to the hardware store like it was some kind of game. Like you wanted to see how hard I would fall for him before he left. Well, I guess you win, because I didn't realize how hard I fell until now."

Carefully, she said, "I just wanted you to be happy. And you *will* be happy again, once this is all sorted out."

There was that word again: *happy*. It baffled me to think of how confident I'd been in the presence of happiness just hours ago. How I'd let the feeling gush over me, unbridled, like the generous spray of a waterfall. Only now did I see that it was actually a faucet during a drought. After reveling in the rush of water, I'd watched it peter out into a steady drip before it dried up completely.

"Did you ever stop to think that maybe my life was easier when I wasn't happy? At least I had nothing to lose."

Her arm fell to her side in defeat, and I seized the opportunity to push past her into the hallway. "Don't do this, Bailey. If anything, you need a support system now more than ever."

I gave her a sidelong glance. "That's what you said last time, remember?" I let the words hang in the air for a moment before turning away. "Thanks for letting me stay at your place, but I've overstayed my welcome. I just can't be in this town anymore. And this time, I mean it."

After finding my way out of the venue, I lingered in the parking lot, scanning the space for Dustin's truck. Stragglers unlocked sedans, SUVs, and pickup trucks, but none of them were his. I stood there until the last fan tore out of the lot, as if his Chevy would materialize out of thin air. As if he would hop out of the cab, arms outstretched, reassuring me that it was all one giant misunderstanding.

I staggered blindly over to a pickup in the corner of the lot and pressed my face against the glass, almost seeing him there behind the wheel, with me sitting beside him. As a sob racked my body, I was carried away in a wave of pain that felt all too familiar. This was the worst kind of pain, the kind that grabbed a person by the throat when they fooled themselves into thinking they were home safe. It was so sudden, so stark compared to the joy I'd felt just moments ago that it almost didn't feel real.

I thought of my younger self and how she thought she knew what happiness was. But she didn't. She never did. Because the joy I'd experienced over these past couple of weeks had exceeded any level I'd imagined.

And the worst part was that I didn't realize it until it was taken away from me.

Chapter 12

I lay in my bed back home the night after the concert, watching the harsh red numbers on my alarm clock announce that it was three thirty in the morning. My eyelids had flown open at three o'clock on the dot, keeping a longstanding tradition alive. Whenever something happened that rattled me, my brain woke me up in the middle of the night to try to make sense of it. It was a cruel wake-up call. In the morning, the daylight helped to absorb some of my pain, muffling it with a blanket of golden light. But the dead of night was the worst time to remember. The thick blackness was a dark screen that projected all my thoughts and fears, where they were impossible to ignore.

Whenever I thought of Dustin, the weight of his absence pressed down on my chest until I could hardly breathe. The only time I found any reprieve was when something else managed to steal my attention for a moment or two. But forgetting was more punitive than thinking about him continuously. As soon as I started to feel a little lighter, my limbs unburdened by the events of that night, I was sucked right back into the tornado. Like a prisoner feeling the fresh air brush her face for a few glorious seconds, only to be thrown back into her cell.

I shut my eyes again and let the snippets of that night float freely through my mind. His misty eyes as he told me he was leaving. The fear that had weighed down his whole body and seeped into his voice. And that one fragment of our short conversation that still echoed through my mind. *But not tonight. Not when you looked happier than I've ever seen you. I can't take that away from you.*

He'd been so afraid of hurting me, he hadn't realized he'd already hurt me by omitting the truth about his family. I thought about all the times he'd withheld something from me, his eyes turning dark whenever I nudged him about his past. Every time he kept a detail to himself, I brushed it off, telling myself he just wasn't ready to share it with me. But that was before we'd been intimate with each other, before I'd let him see me vulnerable. To be shut out after that was the same as being told to my face that I didn't matter. That everything we had up until now was meaningless to him.

I switched on the lamp on my nightstand and pulled out the notebook paper I'd used to scribble down my new songs before the concert. I wasn't sure why I'd brought it with me. Maybe there was a small part of me that hoped creating music would have the power to heal me the way it used to. But I couldn't let myself be that naïve anymore. Anything that brought me joy, whether it was a person or a song, was just as capable of bringing pain. It was best to steer clear of it all before it had the chance to hurt me.

I shoved the paper back into the drawer and switched off the lamp. I lay back down, waiting for sleep that would never come, and thought about returning to the office on Monday. Lauren would be thrilled that I wasn't working remotely anymore and—better yet—that I was setting down my guitar and microphone for the foreseeable future. She was the one who'd delivered that red flare of a warning on the phone: *Do you want to be practical and help other artists achieve their dreams, or do you want to take a one-in-a-million shot at hitting it big? Because when your dreams don't work out, it hurts to know you put your all into them.*

It was the last part of that advice that dug in deep. I *had* put my all into the concert, only to be rewarded with disappointment. Out of all the advice I'd gotten from my family and friends, my boss was the one who'd seen right into the future. And I'd chosen to ignore her.

* * *

I almost didn't hear my phone ringing over the roar of the vacuum. When the peppy tone finally rang out over the noise, I switched off the vacuum and reached for my phone on the counter. My heart rose foolishly, apparently still not having learned its lesson. When I glanced at the screen and didn't see Dustin's name, I silently chastised myself. *Of course it isn't him. Did you really think it would be?*

"Hey, Ev." I didn't realize how exhausted I was until I heard my own voice.

"Before you ask, yes, Cassidy told me everything. So we don't need to get into that. I just wanted to make sure you're okay."

"I'm fine."

"As much as I'd love to believe that answer, I can't."

I turned on the kitchen faucet and started scrubbing away at the few dishes that sat inside the basin. "I'm just doing housework. Life goes on, you know?"

Evelyn sighed. "Look, I'm a lot more cynical than your sister. Probably because I don't live in a cozy little house with the love of my life and two kids running around. So I'm not going to sit here and tell you that everything will be okay. I think what Dustin did to you was wrong. I understand something came up, but that doesn't mean he shouldn't be honest and tell you what's going on. You deserve to know."

"The worst part is that when he told me he was leaving, I just froze. I never got the chance to tell him that he can talk to me about anything, that I would never judge him or change my mind about how I feel. I thought he already knew that, but maybe he didn't. Maybe *I* haven't been open enough with *him*."

"I don't think anything you might have said would've made a difference, to be honest. This is between him and his feelings for you. If he really cares about you, then he'll grow a pair and tell you what's going on. It has to come from him though. You can't force it." She paused. "Have you heard from him at all?"

I shut off the water and placed the dishes on the drying rack. "Not yet. He promised he would call once things were sorted out. Whenever that is."

I collapsed on the couch, having run out of chores to keep my mind occupied. I sat still for a moment as I tried to articulate the web of feelings inside me. "What hurts the most is that I trusted him with my own scars. I told him all about the fire and how I still blame myself for what happened. But he doesn't trust me enough to tell me about his family." I closed my eyes as another wave of exhaustion passed through me. "Just when I started to move on from the last summer concert, this happened. Maybe I never should've performed again. I told myself things would be different this time, but both concerts ended in tears. It doesn't matter if the reasons were different. I'm clearly not meant to be up on stage."

"You're reading way too much into this. It's not the same thing as last time at all. Besides, you had an amazing time. And you saw how happy everyone was for you."

I lay back against the couch cushions and stared at the blank TV. "I should've known this would happen. Everyone goes back to where they came from eventually, and he's a southern boy at heart."

An image appeared in my mind, one so vivid it seemed like it was flashing on the screen in front of me. I saw Dustin sitting at the dining room table in his cozy Georgia cottage, talking and laughing with his extended family while feasting on a traditional home-cooked meal. The shock of whatever had happened had worn off, and he'd decided he wanted to stick around in his hometown for a little while. To be with the people who understood him. His relatives discussed things they had in common with him that I didn't, like their allegiance to the same college football team and their familiarity with the same neighborhood haunts. Afterward, he would retire on the front porch with a cold beer, sitting back and admiring the view he'd left behind so many years ago. I would be far from his mind as he reminisced on old times that I had no part in. Maybe I'd already slipped his thoughts entirely. Maybe he was so deeply entrenched in the thick Georgia clay that he could no longer pry himself free. And maybe he didn't want to. I could see him now, smiling to himself before indulging in another sip, thinking, *Why did I ever leave here in the first place?*

The tears gushed without warning, and it was like a spigot had been turned on. Once I started, I couldn't stop. The pain didn't abate at all with every new attack. Instead, it doused me with the same intensity, like I was reliving the same moment on an endless loop.

Evelyn let me cry, not saying a word. Once I'd calmed down a little, she said, "I'm always here for you. So is your sister. Just remember you can always talk to us when you need to."

I didn't want to talk. I wanted to retreat into myself, burrowing deeper and deeper into my shell where no one could see me. I didn't care what Cassidy said—I handled tough times best on my own. It was everybody's poking and prodding that had ultimately unraveled me six years ago. If they had just let me be, my wounds would have healed faster.

"I just need some time to think things through." I sniffled. "But thanks for calling."

"Of course. Just take care of yourself, okay?"

I lay back down on the couch after the call ended. The bright-green numbers on the oven clock caught my eye: 12:47. Twenty more hours until I returned to work the next morning. But my legs were growing restless, and my mind wouldn't quit its endless rumination. Monday morning seemed terribly far away all of a sudden. I needed to get to work. Now.

I grabbed my bag and headed out the door without thinking too hard about what I was doing. The office would be empty on a Sunday afternoon, which gave me ample time to get organized before my first full day back. My plan seemed more and more appealing as I hopped into the car and started the engine. If chasing joy had left me heartbroken, the only way to survive was to shut joy out of my life completely. And if that meant numbing myself with work, then so be it.

I drove through the quiet suburban town that had once been my refuge, remembering how quickly I'd adjusted to life in Ackerdale. I never thought a free spirit like me would slip so effortlessly into the deep, comfortable grooves of suburbia. I found comfort in the sameness of everything, in the way everyone seemed to follow an invisible script. It was simply easier to be someone I wasn't than to lug around the burden of being myself.

That wasn't to say that I never felt out of place. Sometimes, when I drove by the school and saw the line of minivans snaking toward the pickup lane, I was reminded that I was a single, childless woman—a rare sight in the suburbs. But I tried not to dwell on it too much. I'd learned that if I played the part and kept my head up, people assumed I knew where my place was.

I turned onto Fawn Grove and spotted my neighbor Jackie jogging down the sidewalk in her uniform of pink leggings and a matching sports bra. She huffed and puffed with visible effort despite her slow pace. When she saw my car, she waved at me and jogged up to the driver's side window. I rolled it down as she wrestled her earbuds out of her ears.

Jackie was the first person to make me feel welcome in town when I first moved in. She never badgered me with questions about where my husband was or if I felt lonely in that house all by myself. I loved Jackie for the fact that she preferred rambling on about her own life instead of sticking her nose into mine. And when I was beating myself up over my mistakes or longing for old times, letting Jackie drag me through the mall while rattling off her own inner monologue was the only distraction I needed.

"I didn't know you were coming back," she said by way of greeting. "Let me guess, your sister drove you nuts back home.

I know my sister does. We made life miserable for our poor mother. One minute we'd be peacefully coexisting, and the next we'd be ripping each other's hair out."

I gave her an understanding smile. "Sisters, right?" For a minute, I debated telling her about Dustin. She would probably pull out a story about some guy who'd wronged her to make me feel better. But there was still a chance she would turn the conversation to me, and I was in no mood to entertain her questions.

"You're telling me." She brightened, as if she'd just recalled an old inside joke. "I almost forgot. You remember when I told you that Shaina was starting at Julliard this fall?"

I nodded. That was something else we'd bonded over—her daughter's love for music that echoed my own.

"You won't believe this. She posted a video on YouTube, or I think it was TikTok—whatever kids are using these days—of her covering some Ariana Grande song. And lemme tell you, it *blew up*. Ten million views in less than a week. She's already heard from a couple record companies who are interested in her sound." She beamed like a bird puffing out its feathers. "I guess you can say I'm a proud mama."

Something flared inside me, a white-hot burst of emotion that grabbed hold of me. That could have been me. After the success of my performance at the summer concert, I could have been the one working on a new album and winning the hearts of fans everywhere. But I couldn't bring myself to drive to the studio or play another show. It had taken me six years to come out of my shell again, to take a risk and bare my soul onstage. And I was rewarded with my worst fears coming true a second time.

"I just had to share the news with you, especially after hearing about your concert last night. Maybe you could even give Shaina some tips on making it as a singer. I know she'd be forever grateful."

I strained the corners of my mouth into a smile. "I'd be happy to help."

"Fab!" Jackie glanced down at her Fitbit with a frown. "Still haven't reached my daily goal. Well, I'd better get to it." She gave me an earnest smile. "It's great to have you back, by the way. Greg can really get on my nerves sometimes. I mean, he's my husband—of course I love him. But a girl needs her alone time, you know what I mean?"

I thought about the way I used to feel in the warm circle of Dustin's arms, and a fresh tide of pain rolled through me. I could hardly look at Jackie anymore, this woman who took the security of a loving life partner for granted. One she always found reliably lying by her side when she woke up each morning. She didn't have to worry that he would get up one day and decide he preferred to be in Idaho instead. It was a given that he would be there, every single day, always available for a spontaneous kiss or advice when she needed it most. Yet she had the audacity to say he *got on her nerves*.

I used up all my remaining energy to smile and nod in feigned understanding. I didn't have it in me to drag her down into the dark abyss I was in. Let her stick to her daily fitness goal and come home to her loving but annoying husband and gifted daughter. The world needed more people living structured, predictable lives like her. God knew no one would get anywhere if they were in the state I was in now.

After she jogged away, I opened Spotify and scrolled through my music. I needed something loud enough to scare away the silence that sat in the car like an airtight vacuum. My recommendations were inundated with upbeat, breezy country songs, the kind I used to turn up with the windows down on a balmy afternoon. Just three days ago, Eric had been barbecuing out in the backyard while I played with Leah on the lawn, Kenny Chesney's "Summertime" floating on the breeze. It might as well have been three years ago. The fact that it was still summer never failed to stun me.

I ignored the music that the algorithm was trying to force down my throat and dove deep into the recesses of my library. My finger hovered over a long-forgotten playlist from my teen years, rife with moody album art and angst-ridden lyrics. I played the first song and let the hectic drumbeat pull me into sweet oblivion. It scared me how easily I fell back into that mindset, how effortlessly the darkness blotted out the light I'd worked so hard to attain. It was as if I'd been this way all along, and the past couple of months in Oak Plains were a mirage that I'd mistaken for reality.

As I merged onto the highway, I found myself thinking about Leah and Jade. I'd left my nieces behind almost as suddenly as Dustin had left me. Blinded by my own grief, I hadn't bothered to look beyond their practiced smiles to the hurt I'd likely inflicted upon them. Jade had just started to get along with her mother after I talked to her, and I could tell Leah had grown attached to me as time went by. I swallowed, my throat burning with regret.

I called Cassidy twice, but it went to voicemail both times. It was what I deserved. Six years ago, I'd been the one to leave her texts and calls unanswered. It was high time I got a taste of my own medicine.

I stared blankly at the road that rolled out in front of me like a long gray carpet. Somewhere between Ackerdale and

Pittsburgh, I realized I didn't want to be alone anymore. I wanted my sister to try to console me with her motivational platitudes, of which I swore she had an endless supply. I wanted Evelyn to tell me stories about her many failed dates to convince me that men weren't worth it anyway. I even missed the many casual acquaintances I had scattered throughout Oak Plains, like Anna down at the farm and Ruth across the street. The thought of having a banal conversation with one of those people seemed extraordinarily appealing all of a sudden.

But I'd already made my bed. A bed that was far too big and much too cold for just one person.

Chapter 13

I winced at the sight of my tidy office a week later, convinced it was an impostor who'd kept it so spotless. A few hours after last week's cleaning spree, I'd been overcome with a fatigue that ran deep in my bones. I no longer had it in me to fulfill my plan of becoming Employee of the Year. After the fire, work had been an escape, a chance to push unwanted thoughts out of my mind. Now, it was only a bitter reminder that my life was empty without it.

If Lauren could see this attitude written on my face, she didn't say anything about it. Instead, she'd greeted me on the day of my return with an outward look of self-satisfaction, just like I'd predicted. "Nashville didn't have a spot for you, huh?" Her voice was pleased, almost melodic. With my sweetest smile, I said, "They did, but I turned it down. I don't need to be in the spotlight to make music. Besides, who wants to deal with paparazzi and crazed fans? No thanks."

I saw her eye twitch just before I disappeared into my office, and I knew my lie had hit a sore spot. To her, that was worse than hearing I was on my way to superstardom. To think I'd turned down an opportunity that she would have done anything for—that was pure agony.

If I started off on the wrong foot, I spent the rest of the week walking a mile on it. I was finishing up my lunch break the following Monday when I ran into a scrawny, freckled boy in his late teens, a guitar case strapped optimistically across his back. I saw the sheen of hope in his eyes, the kind of hope I'd nurtured on the night of the concert. Looking at him, I only saw the crushing disappointment he would feel when his dreams eventually came apart at the seams. He would learn later on that it was better not to hold on too tightly to something that was never meant to be his in the first place. I knew all too well that the earlier he found out, the better.

"Excuse me," he said. "Do you know where I can find Lauren? I have a meeting with her at one thirty."

"She's on her lunch break now. She should be back soon." I should have stopped there, but I couldn't help myself. I studied him for a moment. "Let me guess. You sent in your demo, and she already thinks you're exploding with potential."

He blushed. That sweet, sensitive look on his face, coupled with his mop of brown curls, made me think of Shawn Mendes. "Something like that, yeah."

I did my best to look unimpressed. "We get people like you all the time around here. I wouldn't get your hopes up about this meeting, to be honest. You're going to have to really stand out to get Lauren to sign you."

A brief flicker of disappointment darkened his face, but he quickly traded it for a look of feigned confidence. "I've been practicing for years, and I think all my hard work is about to pay off. I got this."

He sounded like he was trying to convince himself more than me. I rested a consolatory hand on his shoulder. "Practice can only get you so far, you know. You're probably better off keeping your music to yourself."

He stared at me blankly, like he wasn't sure which emotion to choose. I threw a bright smile over my shoulder and returned to my desk, feeling perversely triumphant. My job here was done. One less broken heart to worry about.

A couple of hours later, Lauren called me into her office to deliver a warning. Apparently, telling a potential client to give up on his dreams wasn't good for business. Which meant keeping me around would only hold back said business if I continued with my behavior.

I knew I'd set myself up for disaster the minute I stepped into the office. But it didn't hit me how close I'd come to losing my job until I gathered my things to leave at the end of the day.

So much had transpired over the past week that it felt like I was stuck in one of those nonsensical dreams I had when I was in and out of sleep. I even felt unsteady as I crossed the parking lot, as if I weren't real. Just a dream avatar moving aimlessly about, fulfilling meaningless tasks until the real me woke up and resumed her actual life.

I was making my way up my front steps when Cassidy's name flashed across my phone screen. I sat down on the single wicker chair that adorned my front porch and hit Accept. "Hey," I said hesitantly, not quite sure where we stood.

"Hey. My sister senses were telling me something was up, so I had to call."

"Well, you're right about that." I gazed up at the spotless sky, so blue it was almost cartoonish. "I almost got fired today."

"You *what*? What did you do?"

"I told a potential client that it isn't worth it to pursue a music career."

"Oh, Bailey." I could feel her trying to keep her emotions under control but failing. "Are you out of your mind?"

"I did him a favor. Isn't it better to be warned about failure than to have it just slap you in the face when you least expect it? He'll be thanking me one day."

"I didn't think you were this bad." She let out a long breath. "Things are going to happen, Bailey. People are going to disappoint you. You're going to have bad times mixed in with the good. You can't just avoid everything that makes you happy because it might let you down. That's not living."

When I didn't respond, she said, "The problem is that you see everything as the end. But we healed after the fire, and Dustin will come back to you. I know you know that deep down, but you're too stubborn to let hope inside. You're doing the same thing you did six years ago—putting up a shield in front of your feelings. You might think it's easier to shut out hope so you won't be let down, but that's no way to live."

"That's not true. I might not be as optimistic as you, but I'm not that bad." Even as I said the words, fear sat like a brick in my stomach. My lack of trust for Dustin, my turning my back on music—I couldn't ignore how the fortress I'd built around my heart was robbing me of all the parts of life I cherished most. Before it sank in too far, I banished the thought from my mind.

"It is that bad if it's the reason you're giving up on Dustin. I know you think he's gone forever, but my gut is never wrong about this stuff. You're seeing everything through the lens of your fear, and it's making you blind to the person Dustin really is."

"He already showed me who he is by not trusting me to let me into such a big part of his life. And by cutting me out completely for the past week," I pointed out. "Wasn't it you who said that a person shows their true character through their actions? Well, that's exactly what he did."

In the silence that followed, I could tell Cassidy was making a great effort to be patient with me. After a beat, she said, "Do you know the moment that I knew Eric was right for me? There weren't any fireworks or fanfare like there are in the movies. We were just sitting together on the couch one night and I felt... safe. The kind you feel in your bones. Like I knew he'd be there for me for the rest of my life. There were plenty of other things that didn't make sense in my life at that time, but I knew for sure that he was the only person I'd ever be happy with."

I tried to remember having a moment like that with Dustin, but the storm he'd brought me overshadowed all of the light he'd once shone into my life. "So what are you saying? That I need to wait for that magical feeling to come?"

"I'm saying you'll know if he doesn't love you. There won't be any room for doubt. If you really do trust him, you won't see this as the end. Just a rough patch that you'll work through somehow."

For what must have been the tenth time since that Saturday, Dustin's words to me echoed through my thoughts. *Maybe one day I'll be ready to let you into that part of my life, but not tonight.* His internal struggle had been written on his face, and it was clear that the desire to tell me the truth had lost out to an unseen rival. It occurred to me then that I wanted to trust him, even when I thought I'd been drained of all hope. But I couldn't let myself do it.

Hearing my sister's voice turned my attention away from Dustin, and it soon wandered to the two souls I'd left behind back home. I drew in a slow breath. "So... how are Jade and Leah?"

She let out a loud huff. "Jade isn't doing so great. You don't understand this yet because you don't have kids, but a child of that age needs someone to look up to. I'm just her frumpy old mother, so she looks right past me. But you're the young, hip aunt who gives great advice and is into the same kind of music as her. You were becoming a role model to her, in a way. But then you just picked up and left, and... Well, Jade's even worse off now than she was before."

A lump wedged itself into my throat. It was everything I hadn't wanted to hear. "What about Leah?"

"Well, you know Leah. Always trying to put a brave face on. But I know her better than anyone, and I can tell she feels the same way as her sister."

"I'm so sorry. But you knew I wasn't going to stick around forever, right? It isn't even my home anymore."

"It'll always be your home, Bailey. You saw how everyone welcomed you with open arms as soon as you came back."

"Jackie was happy to see me when I came back to Ackerdale," I pointed out, my voice unusually defensive.

"You never even liked Jackie." She sighed. "Just do me a favor and don't forget who you are while you're gone."

Before I could respond, I was met with dead air. I sighed and fixed my gaze on the blue blanket above me, wondering how the sky had the audacity to look so cheerful. Loneliness weighed down on my chest as I watched a pair of children frolicking in the yard a few houses down. I couldn't sit here by myself. Not right now.

Ignoring what my sister had said about Jackie, I pulled out my phone and sent a quick text to my friend. I knew she could never turn down a mall trip. It wasn't in her blood. Besides, she needed an excuse to get away from her annoying husband. I tensed up as I recalled her flippant comment about Greg.

Jackie turned up at my house in under ten minutes. She poked her head out the window of her minivan and lowered her sunglasses. "Why didn't you tell me earlier that you wanted to hit up the mall? My fat ass needs a new pair of jeans." She rolled her eyes. "I swear, if Greg keeps tempting me with his homemade bread, I'm gonna need to buy a whole new wardrobe."

I stifled a groan as I slid into the passenger seat. This was going to be a long ride if she insisted on talking about her husband the whole time.

"So," she said, pulling out of the drive, "you won't believe what happened after I finished my run this morning. I was doing some laundry, or at least *trying* to, because Greg just leaves his dirty clothes in random spots all over the house. It's like a freakin' scavenger hunt. Anyway, I'm just putting in the first load when I get a call from Shaina's teacher. She actually has the nerve to tell me that my Shaina is being *disruptive* in class. It's so obvious the problem is the kids around her who won't leave her alone. I tried to explain that to her teacher, but she wouldn't have any of it…"

My mind drifted off as Jackie droned on about the school system failing her daughter, who could apparently do no wrong. Normally, I would have welcomed any opportunity to engage in mindless chitchat with my friend. But it had no effect on me now. As I watched miles of suburban sprawl blur past me, I realized I felt just as lonely as I had before I'd called Jackie.

In a rare moment of perceptiveness, she eyed me with her lower lip folded into a pout. "You look sad," she said, like a kindergartener matching the correct emotion to the picture.

When I shrugged, she raised her eyebrows. "Is it guy trouble?"

"Sort of."

She shook her head. "And here I am, going on and on about my husband. You could've said something, you know."

There was more self-awareness in those words than in all the time I'd known her. It made me feel like I owed her a small tidbit of information in return.

"It's just a guy I knew back home. We kind of started something together, but I don't think it's going anywhere."

"Aww, don't say that. You never know what's going to happen. I never told you this, but things weren't always smooth sailing with Greg in the beginning. We had our differences, and all my friends did a pretty good job of pointing them out to me. But I didn't let any of that get in the way of my feelings for him. And it was so worth it. *He* was so worth it."

"You've never mentioned that," I said quietly. "It just seems like he drives you crazy all the time."

She looked at me like she was talking to a naïve child. "Of course he does sometimes. And I'm sure I do too. But if I never saw his dirty shirts hanging over the armchair again, I would be heartbroken. You'll know what I mean when you find your own Greg."

I felt a dull ache in my gut. Jackie had her Greg, just like Cassidy had her Eric. A possessive pronoun tossed about so carelessly, the way someone could only do when they were secure in their love for another person. There was no questioning whether someone else out there was better suited to them. They just *knew*—as surely as they knew the weather or the color of their shirt.

"This is perfect timing, because you totally need some retail therapy right now." Right on cue, Jackie turned into the parking lot of the Wellsford County Mall. The sight of the behemoth structure in all its capitalist glory wrapped me in a warm blanket of comfort. It was the way I used to feel when I sought refuge in the woods or on my sunlit back porch, and I couldn't help but wonder if I was slowly turning into Jackie.

The inside of the mall was unrecognizable from the way it looked during the typical weekend rush. Only a few shoppers were scattered here and there, most of them walking quickly and with purpose. It was a noticeable difference from the crowds that tended to linger on weekends. Even the food court was eerily quiet, with gooey slices of pizza and fat, golden-brown pretzels sitting untouched under heat lamps.

Jackie whisked her way through the maze of stores like she was in her own home. As we rode the escalator up to the third floor, she studied the shops above us with a practiced eye. "I was thinking about popping into Nordstrom for a sec." She shot me a look. "Don't let me stay there for more than ten minutes. I'm serious. Even if you have to drag me out."

We got off the escalator and started to head toward Nordstrom. Halfway there, she came to an abrupt halt in front of the Bath & Beauty Shop. "Oh, crap. You know I can't resist this place." As she entered the store, I debated keeping her on track but decided it was easier to just let her be.

She began sampling the various scented candles and lotions while I hung back and tried to find something remotely appealing. Just a cursory glance at the labels—Tropical Dream, Strawberry Shortcake—told me everything in the store was too cloyingly sweet for my liking. I was waving away an unwelcome puff of cherry blossom body spray when Jackie approached me, a bottle of lavender perfume in hand. "Can you tell me what you think of this one? I need someone with a good nose."

"I think my sense of smell is currently in overdrive, but I'll give it a shot." I took the bottle from her and sprayed the perfume on my wrist. Just as I caught a whiff, a female voice filtered through the speaker on the ceiling. It was so familiar it almost felt like it was a part of me. Only after a moment or two did I realize it was my own.

They were playing "Down This Country Road" on the radio. The first single from *Wanderlust*, the album I'd recorded six years ago. After so many years of tirelessly honing my craft and trying to make a name for myself, I'd achieved a dream I never thought would become reality. My song being aired on a professional radio station for all of the Northeast to hear.

I should have been elated. I should have been celebrating with Cassidy and Evelyn. I should have been running over to Dustin's house to share the news so he could pick me up and twirl me in the air like he'd done before the concert. Instead, I was standing in the middle of a store I hated with a woman who probably didn't even know the name of the song that was playing.

Her eyes widened. "That's you, isn't it?"

I had to give her some points for knowing that much. I forced a smile. "It's a song I recorded years ago." I had to pause and swallow before speaking again. "'Down This Country Road.'"

"That's amazing! I'd say this is cause for celebration." She started scanning the shelves and grabbed a large candle labeled Best Wishes. "You should take this home. The scent is to die for." Before I could refuse, she pulled out her wallet and started walking to the register. "Don't worry. It's on me."

Chapter 13

I watched her pay for a candle I didn't want while my voice continued to drift out of the speaker. It sounded just as dreamy and hopeful as the girl who'd recorded the song all those years ago. I hardly even recognized the person I'd been back then.

It wasn't until we were crossing the parking lot to Jackie's minivan that a heavy sadness pressed down on my chest. Despite what I told myself about being okay with the way I was living now, I knew deep down that I wanted to be that girl again. No matter how big the risk was.

Chapter 14

That day at the mall wasn't the last time I heard my song on the radio. A week later, I was flipping through the stations on my way to work when I landed on a local country station. When I heard my voice accompanied by the pluck of a banjo, I cursed under my breath and reached over to shut off the radio. Ever since my performance Saturday night, newly proclaimed fans of mine had been unearthing songs from my first album and touting them as sleeper hits. That shot of a younger, more innocent me surrounded by wildflowers popped up in random places when I least expected it.

It was a cruel joke that my album was finally getting the recognition I'd craved now that music had abandoned me again. My throat had closed up, afraid of what misfortune would befall me if I ventured to sing again. The vague melody that was always coursing through my mind, an ever-present work in progress, had been silenced. I was even beginning to find that I preferred this state of nothingness, this autopilot setting I'd chosen. Numbness was like a layer of insulation over my emotions. It muffled the pain, but in doing so, it also blocked out any possibility of happiness.

I walked into the building and set my things down on my desk. Ever since I'd gotten in trouble for shattering a client's hopes and dreams, I'd decided it would be better for everyone if I detached myself from my work. I needed to stop seeing the girl I used to be in the eyes of every aspiring musician who crossed my path. I needed to stop hearing my own voice in every demo I listened to. My own career was long over. It was time to start focusing my energy on the careers of the musicians I was here to mentor.

Danielle, the receptionist, popped her head into my office barely five minutes later. "I have Callie Adams here to see you." She seemed to falter for a moment before continuing. "Um, and Lauren wanted to make sure I told you to keep it professional this time."

I strained all my face muscles into a smile as Callie power walked into the room, and I couldn't help comparing her to the cowering version of Madison who'd entered my office that first time. As Callie took a seat across from me, I tried to call her sound to mind. I'd listened to so many demos since the concert that they were all starting to blur together.

"So, what did you think of my song?" she asked, unprompted.

Her overconfident tone immediately filled the gaps in my memory. She was the one who'd boldly asserted in her pitch that she was going to redefine country music. Her demo suggested as much. There were no mentions of one-stoplight towns, pickup trucks, scuffed-up cowboy boots, or any of the usual themes that populated the genre. Quite the opposite, actually.

Her electric guitar-heavy ballad told the story of a girl who hated everything about her backward town and longed to trade it in for a more ambitious life in the big city. Which was admirable but defeated the whole purpose of her chosen genre.

I hesitated, unsure how to express all of that to her without breaking her heart. I didn't need a repeat of my encounter with the Shawn Mendes look-alike. "It was definitely unique," I began. "And it takes guts to take any kind of artistic risk, so I give you props for that."

"But?" she broke in.

I gave her a tight smile. "Let me put it this way. Fans of any type of music have specific expectations that they carry with them, whether they're aware of it or not. If you market a song as country, they're going to expect it to sound a certain way. Your song strays too far from what country fans want. We certainly welcome new ideas, but they still have to fit into the conventions of the genre."

She crossed her arms, suddenly defiant. "Plenty of people have told me that my music is a breath of fresh air. I mean, how many songs can you listen to about never wanting to leave your small town? It gets boring after a while."

"But that's what people love about that kind of music. If you rebel against everything that draws people to the genre, you can't really call it country anymore."

"At least I'm not a poser," she muttered.

"Excuse me?"

"I read on your fan page that you left your hometown and moved out to the suburbs. But you still sing songs about country roads and farms and everything you left behind. At least I'm not trying to be someone I'm not."

Her cutting tone sliced right through me, but I didn't dare

let her know it. Instead, I remembered what Danielle had told me about staying professional. "I recorded those songs when I still lived in my hometown. A lot has happened since then, and that's why I haven't released a new album in years. But I'm only interested in your music right now. And I don't think your sound is the right fit for us."

"You're missing out on a big opportunity, then. It's always the trailblazers who end up being the most successful."

She started to go, but I stopped her. "Wait. Why did you read my fan page if you don't even like the kind of music I make?"

Her eyes rested on me for a long moment before she spoke. "I might not like your music, but you're obviously talented. And if there's one thing I learned from all the haters, it's that you should never let talent go to waste, even if other people don't like it. Which is why I'm going to find another label that believes in my music." With that, she turned and walked out of the room.

I sat there with my head in my hands after Callie had left. She was right. I was wasting my talent. And the worst part was that I wasn't doing anything about it. Callie might have just faced rejection, but at least she'd tried. I was simply letting defeat silence me, just like I had six years ago.

I couldn't keep waiting for my life to get better before I started singing again. I needed to use what I was going through now to shape my music—no matter how messy it got. And I needed to start today.

I pulled out my phone and sent a quick text to Dan, a sound technician who worked at the studio and was good friends with Evelyn. He was the one who'd coached me through the recording process and helped me make my first album a reality. Even though I lacked a clear idea of what I would be working on, I still felt butterflies of excitement rustling in my stomach.

I could go wherever I wanted with this recording session. And the best part was that I hadn't even decided on a destination yet.

I set down my phone and got to work. With the idea of crafting a new song filling me with energy, I powered through my to-do list for that day faster than usual. At this rate, I would be able to sneak out of work early and get a head start on my next song.

When my phone rang ten minutes later, I smiled, knowing Dan had already booked a slot for me at the studio. "Hey. Got everything set up?"

There was a lengthy pause. Then: "Bailey, it's me."

My heart did such a big jump that I had to catch my breath. I yanked the phone away from my ear and stared at his name on the screen, wondering if it was a figment of my imagination. I hadn't even bothered looking at the caller ID, because I didn't think this would happen. Not after two weeks of complete silence.

"Dustin?" I said, my voice a wisp of itself.

"I need to talk to you. Is this a good time?"

I never knew it was possible to feel such immense joy at hearing someone's voice again but want to hang up on them at the same time. After he'd made me second-guess myself and whittled away at my trust little by little, I couldn't give in to him that easily. Despite how much I ached to speak to him again, I needed him to feel the sting of what he'd done to me. Even though it would never measure up to what I'd felt that night.

"I'm at work now. I have a lot to do."

"Bailey, please let me explain. I didn't tell you what was really going on that night, but I'm willing to tell you everything now if you're willing to listen."

I paused for a brief moment to steady my voice. "Where were you the past two weeks? You could've at least texted me."

"I've been doing a lot of thinking about us and about that night. Trying to find the right words to say. And I finally have them."

"Do you know what I haven't been able to get out of my head since that night?" I asked, fighting back tears. "You thought telling me about your family would ruin my perfect night. But guess what? It's the other way around. The only thing that ruined my night was you keeping the truth from me."

"I wasn't ready to tell you the truth then. But I am now, if you'll let me explain."

I shook my head even though he couldn't see me. "You still don't understand. You think you can just omit the truth when it's uncomfortable for you and then come clean as soon as it's convenient again. That's not how it works. If you're not open with me all the time, how am I ever supposed to trust you? How do I know you're not just getting my hopes up so you can stomp all over them again?"

"Because I would never do that to you." I could feel him growing more frantic with every word.

"You already did. And until you understand how you made me feel, anything you say to me won't matter."

I ended the call before he could respond. Hearing his voice again had reopened the wound he'd left in his wake. Now I had to sit with the pain of his disappearance all over again. With a sinking feeling, I realized he'd never mentioned when he was coming back. Or if he was coming back at all. I tried to remind myself that it didn't matter, because we weren't in a position to reunite anyway. But that didn't make the weight of his absence any less oppressive.

I knew if Cassidy had seen his number flash onto my screen, she would've already started celebrating. It was that easy for her. *See? I told you he would come around,* she would say. But Evelyn saw the world without the gaudy sheen of optimism that blinded my sister's judgment. She was the one I needed to talk to about this.

I waited until after work to call her. I headed into the living room and perched on the couch. "Guess who showed up out of the blue today?"

"My future husband?"

"No. Dustin."

She drew in a sharp breath. "Wait, you saw him? So he came back home?"

"He called me and said he wants to explain everything that happened that night. But why didn't he say it before? That's what's eating away at me. The fact that he completely shut me out and practically forgot I existed for two weeks."

Evelyn was quiet for a second. "So, you didn't let him explain?"

"No." I ran a hand through my hair. "Maybe I should have, but I was just so frustrated with him. It was like telling me what happened wasn't even an option for him that night. And that hurt like hell. I tried to tell him that, but I still don't think he gets it."

She sighed. "I swear, you're making single life look better and better every day."

Normally, I would've at least cracked a smile at that, but I didn't have it in me this time. "What should I do?"

"Well, I can't tell you what to do. You know his heart better than I do. I just want to make sure you're making choices based on what you think is right and not based on your fear of disappointment."

Her words gave me pause. Was I really acting out of fear? Or was I right to keep my distance after the way he'd treated me?

"I just want the old Dustin back," I said softly. "The one who always had a smile on his face and a new adventure planned every time we saw each other. I could never see that Dustin just running away and going radio silent on me."

There was a pause. "You mean the way you did?"

"What are you talking about?"

"When you left Oak Plains after the fire. You didn't warn any of us. You got out of town while the smell of smoke was still in the air. How do you think Cassidy and Jade and I felt when you did that? How do you think *Dustin* felt?"

I bristled. "That's not the same thing at all. We weren't even in a relationship then. We barely knew each other."

"That's not the point. The point is that you hurt him, just like he hurt you. But he didn't hold that against you when you came back to town. He welcomed you with open arms like you never even left. I know what he did was wrong, but the ball's in your court now. It's up to you to let him back into your life. Or not."

I opened my mouth to say something, but she spoke before I had the chance. "I have to go. But I really hope you think hard about all this."

After she ended the call, I noticed there was a hollow feeling in the pit of my stomach. No one was going to hold my hand and walk me through this. I had to figure it out on my own.

Before I could let the feeling daunt me, I reminded myself that I was no stranger to doing things on my own. I'd built my music career on my own. I'd created a new life outside of Oak Plains on my own. This wasn't any different. I just needed the right attitude to get to where I wanted to be.

In my bedroom, I pulled an old notebook out of the top drawer of my nightstand, the ink-laden pages still reminding me of the songbook I'd lost. Flipping through my songbook had been like reading a journal peppered with my innermost thoughts and feelings. Anything I didn't dare say aloud, I documented inside those thin, worn pages. Even though I didn't have the original notebook with me anymore, I could start fresh with this one. A tribute to the fresh start in my music career.

I opened up to a blank page, which mocked me with its emptiness. I had a session booked at the studio the next day, and I still didn't have a song to sing. I needed to stop overthinking things. I needed to let everything I was feeling flow out of me like the music flowed out of my guitar. Whatever ideas popped into my mind, I would run free with them.

I wrote and strummed my guitar with a new kind of fervor, one I hadn't felt since the day I wrote my first song in six years. As I brought my music to life, I realized I was unleashing all the words I wanted to say to Dustin but couldn't. Somehow, it was easier to say them under the veil of a song than to say them outright to him.

When I was done, I read through the lyrics and played the song again. It was unlike anything else I'd sung before. There was an edginess to my voice, an angst embedded in the notes that sounded more grunge than country. The majority of my songs were the product of happy times: a beautiful summer day, an exciting life event, or even just a quiet joy that warmed my insides. I tended to bury the bad times instead of letting them rise to the surface in the form of a song. But maybe taking a different path was just what I needed. Maybe creating something out of pain instead of joy would help me heal. And—I could only hope—my fans would understand my artistic vision and be just as excited about it as I was.

The thought of upgrading my sound filled me with an energy that I could no longer hold inside. The world needed to hear this new version of me and needed to hear it now. Not only had it been years since I'd released my first album, but my old sound was unrecognizable compared to the one I'd just crafted. Just thinking about introducing my fans to this new side of me made me want to hop into my car and drive to the studio.

As I set down my guitar, I told myself I didn't need Evelyn to accompany me this time. I needed to follow my own instincts if I was going to make my new sound as authentic as possible. And if that meant going at it alone, then that was the way it had to be.

I placed the notebook back in my drawer and started dreaming about all the other directions that were open to me. The options were endless. And they were all mine for the taking.

Chapter 15

I stood in front of the microphone in the recording studio the next morning, warming up my voice. I was slated to oversee Madison's recording session at eleven o'clock. Madison was the artist Lauren had chosen to sign after the concert, which meant I would be directly involved in the production of her debut album. In the meantime, though, I had a couple hours to focus on my own sound until Madison came in.

As an A&R coordinator, the only reason I stepped foot into a professional studio these days was to assist other musicians with the recording process. The familiar environment somehow felt more daunting when I was the one facing the mic. Dan, the sound technician I'd texted the other day, had helped me eventually overcome my nerves. Now, I focused solely on the quality of my voice, working hard to prepare it for my first recording session in years.

Chapter 15

In the calm solitude of the studio, thoughts of Dustin were far from my mind. When I was with my music, it was like I was exempt from the real world, at least for a little while. Nothing existed between the soundproof walls except the sound of my art.

"You ready?" Dan asked.

I nodded, and my band started to play the intro of the song. I closed my eyes and lost myself in the music, the opening melody propelling me into the first verse. Once I'd built up the momentum I needed, I jumped into the lyrics I'd written in my room. I experienced every emotion all over again as I ran through the verse. I felt it all—the betrayal, the anger, the hurt—as acutely as I did when I penned the song. Hearing all those emotions saturated in my voice was a cathartic feeling. I was setting them free, letting them run wild. I felt better than I had in a long time.

I'd just begun the chorus when Lauren burst into the room. My voice broke off as I caught sight of my boss standing there, glowering at me. In a sharp, clipped tone, she said, "You're supposed to be with Madison now."

I eyed the clock above the door. "It's only nine thirty. She's not coming in until eleven."

Her eye twitched, and that was when it all fell into place. Carving out time to nurture my own craft was off-limits. I was supposed to be like my boss, helping people chase their dreams while my own dreams withered away in a cobwebbed corner.

"Excuse me, ma'am," Dan said. "Recording is in session now."

Now, poor Dan was the victim of her merciless glare. "I'm the manager of Mountain Lion Records. I'm well aware that Bailey was recording. I came in here to remind her that she has another job to do."

I smiled. "Glad you've finally met Dan, Lauren. He helped me record my first album." I turned to him. "You remember, right?"

"Course," he said.

Lauren's stare lingered on my face for a beat too long. "You recorded an *album?*"

I nodded. "I can send you a copy, if you'd like."

My boss's gaze flicked between the two of us before landing on me again. "Can I speak to you outside for a second?"

I shrugged at Dan and followed Lauren into the parking lot. The wind whipped her fine blond strands every which way, and the sunlight softened her blue-green eyes. For a moment, she stood there silently, her mind somewhere far away. When she finally faced me again, she said, "You know, I used to be just like you not too long ago."

I squinted into the sun. "Like me how?"

"I wanted exactly what you want. I dreamed of making country music that everyone loved. I saved up for my own guitar and everything." She shook her head and smiled in the nostalgic way that older people did when they reflected on the good old days. "I played that thing all day long when I was in high school. My mom threatened to take it away from me if my grades kept dropping. I'm pretty sure the only reason I made an effort to do well in school was so I could keep playing."

"That does sound like me," I said, smiling.

"Except you've already done so much more than I ever could've done. I never even made it into a studio. Well, except to fulfill my label manager duties." She peered into my face. "I guess I just have flashbacks of my younger self when I see you sing. It makes me think of the famous country singer I never had the chance to be."

I thought of what Eric had said when I'd told him about Lauren's blowup at my concert appearance: *It's easy to become bitter when you see someone basking in even a fraction of the fame you wish you had.* Looking at my boss now, I saw her in a different light. She wasn't out to get me. I'd just reopened an old wound of hers, causing all the blood to seep out anew.

"It's not too late, you know."

She gave me a dubious look. "I must have a really good makeup routine then, because I'm pushing fifty. You see all the kids making music on TikTok these days. They're barely out of the womb. You've got to start young or else no one cares."

She considered me for a moment. "By the way, what was that song you were working on in there? It didn't sound like anything I've heard from you."

"I was in the mood to try something different, so I just ran with it. I'm not really sure where it's going yet, but I'm open to pretty much anything."

She leaned against the side of the building and crossed her arms, looking at me thoughtfully. "You should ramp it up a bit. Nothing sells like an emotionally charged song. Ever hear Olivia Rodrigo's music?"

I nodded.

"You need to channel that anger, just like Olivia does. And Alanis Morrissette and everyone else who came before her."

I mulled over this. She made a good point, but how would my fans react to such a drastic change in sound? It was one thing to take a creative risk like I'd done in the studio, but it was another thing entirely to change who I was as an artist. It was too big of a leap, especially when I'd just started getting the attention I wanted.

But maybe it was worth it. This was, after all, my chance to unveil my true feelings to Dustin. If he didn't hear me before, he would hear me loud and clear now.

I smiled at Lauren. "I might just take your advice. Thanks."

"Anytime. Good luck."

Feeling like I'd just been reborn, I reemerged into the studio. I took my place at the microphone and turned to Phil, my guitarist. "Go a little heavier on the guitar this time."

He looked uncertain. "You sure?"

"Positive."

He shrugged and started to strum the same chords, only louder and with more intensity. I closed my eyes and let the crunch of the guitars rumble through me like thunder. This was why I made music. So I could step out of myself for a little while and be whoever I wanted to be. The microphone was my paintbrush, giving me the power to mold myself into the type of person I chose to become.

After I wrapped up the song, a thrill shot through my veins. I spotted Lauren out of the corner of my eye, a satisfied smile resting comfortably on her face. Before I could figure out what it meant, she was already gone.

* * *

After finishing up my recording session with Madison in the early afternoon, I drove home in silence. Hearing her sing reminded me of the music I used to make before I decided to reinvent myself. But instead of making me second-guess my decision, the session had fueled my resolve to go in a completely different direction. Madison's fans would grow tired of her music eventually. It happened all the time to anyone who produced art. By constantly reshaping my sound, I could stay one step ahead of everyone else. People would have no choice but to pay attention to me, whether they wanted to or not.

I got out of the car and started fumbling with my house keys. I'd just stepped inside the front hallway when an unknown number flashed across my phone screen. I dropped my bag onto the couch and examined the number, which began with the familiar string of digits that was my hometown's area code. Warily, I hit Accept. "Hello?"

"Bailey? It's Anna Cooke." Her words rushed together into a single breath. "Your sister gave me your number after I heard what was going on down at the hardware store."

"What happened?"

"Dustin's dad hasn't shown up in weeks. He put Ron and the other guys in charge, but the whole place is falling apart without him. I know his health hasn't been great lately, so I wanted to call you to see if you knew anything. Since you and Dustin are an item now and everything."

My mind spun as I tried to make sense of her words. I had the sneaking suspicion that Dustin's disappearance was somehow related to his father's medical condition. But if his dad's health was in trouble, why would he run off to Georgia when his dad needed him most? Something wasn't adding up.

"Well, Dustin and I haven't exactly been on great terms lately."

"Oh. Are you not together anymore?"

"Technically we still are, but… it's complicated. Ever since he left for Georgia, things have been kind of weird between us."

There was a beat of silence before Anna asked, "Do you think his dad is there too?"

Tiny pinpricks of moisture broke out across my forehead, as if my body were sensing danger before I did. "I didn't think of that. What if something happened to him?"

"I don't know, Bailey, but I don't have a good feeling about this. You should really talk to Dustin. I'm sure he has a lot to tell you."

I bit down on my lip, knowing she was right. This wasn't about him leaving anymore. This was about him reaching out to me while I refused to take his hand.

Just a quick call. It didn't mean I was letting him into my life again. I just wanted to make sure everything was okay.

"All right. I'll talk to him."

"Thank goodness," she said, releasing a breath. "Please keep me in the loop."

"I will."

I switched to my contacts and found his name. My heart beat restlessly as I waited for him to answer. The ringing went on and on, each ring somehow louder than the last. I could have simply caught him at a bad time. But the alternatives were plentiful. Maybe he'd given up waiting for me. Maybe whatever was keeping him busy back home had robbed him of the space in his mind where I used to be. Maybe he'd been inconsolable at first, the pain of whatever happened too much for him to bear. But it wouldn't take long for a cute girl to offer her tanned shoulder to him, to dry his tears with her bleached-blond waves. She would perfectly fit the space I used to fill. Except with her, there was no translation necessary. They both spoke the same language of the South, both read the same map of their hometown. They understood each other. More than someone like me could ever understand someone like him.

I hung up without leaving a message and buried my head in my hands. Every scenario I conjured in my mind was just as likely as the next one. And not knowing what was true made this all even more painful.

Chapter 16

Waking up and knowing that my single was out in the world was an odd feeling. It was a feeling I hadn't experienced since I released my first album. Back then, though, I only had a fraction of the fan base I had now. It was a whole different story when a full-fledged audience was eagerly awaiting my next move.

I was just finishing up lunch when my phone dinged with a text from Jackie: *Have you seen this???*

She'd attached a link to an article from Country Music Today, an online publication that covered lesser-known country artists as well as all the bigger stars in the industry. I spotted my name in the URL along with the title of my single, "Bitter." My pulse started to quicken. I realized I was holding my breath as I opened the link.

The headline jumped out at me in bold, accusing letters: *Bailey Flynn's New Single Leaves a "Bitter" Taste in Fans' Mouths.* I bet they were pleased with their clever play on words. Trying to ignore the dread that was ballooning in my gut, I scrolled down and read the first paragraph.

Bailey Flynn took fans by surprise this morning when she unexpectedly dropped a brand-new single. Devoted listeners were probably expecting another upbeat tune from the Pennsylvania native when they heard the news. Little did they know she had something very different up her sleeve. The angsty, electric-guitar-infused hit sounds like it belongs in a late-2000s Paramore album and has fans worried. Is this just a sign of healthy experimentation, or is it signaling a more permanent change in Bailey's sound?

I continued scrolling until I reached the bottom of the article, where the author had pettily included a string of unfavorable tweets about my song. Already cringing, I read a few of them:

I waited five years for this?? WTF. If I wanted Avril Lavigne, I would've bought tickets to her concert back in 2006.

Is Bailey having an early midlife crisis or something, because then I never want to be 28.

This is worse than when Taylor Swift went full-blown pop. Country music is dead, y'all.

The last tweet had garnered the most likes and retweets. Overall, the consensus seemed to be that I'd betrayed my own genre by releasing the song. Was it that unforgivable to step out of my self-inflicted box for once?

I tapped on the messages app and fired off a text to Jackie: *Thanks for sharing, but it's NBD. Focusing on the haters gets you nowhere.*

Her response came almost instantly: *Wow. Respect. If that happened to me, I'd be an absolute mess right now.*

I blinked. Something about her tone made me aware of the magnitude of what had just happened. In a sudden need for an ego boost, I started hunting down the positive reactions to my song, which were surely hidden beneath all the debris of criticism. It wasn't worth using up all my energy on people who didn't believe in what I did.

I combed through various websites and social media platforms, but it was like stepping into an echo chamber. Everyone seemed to be equally horrified by my latest release. If there were any dissenters, their thoughts were drowned out by the less-forgiving majority. It was getting harder and harder to put a positive spin on what was undoubtedly a huge mistake.

Now that my big comeback had unraveled before my eyes, I felt lost. I hadn't realized how much I'd been counting on my plan to work until now. Without the success of my song to lean on, the cold reality of my loneliness sat naked in the harsh, unforgiving light. And I didn't like what I saw at all.

I grabbed my phone and called Cassidy before I could give it another thought. Even after all these years, my instinct was still to turn to my sister whenever I was in a dark place. It was like we understood each other on a different level, one that I could never achieve with Evelyn or anyone else I was close to.

"Hey," she greeted, her voice sounding worn down.

"Hey. I'm guessing you heard what everyone's saying about my new single."

"This may shock you, but no, I haven't. I have two kids to worry about. Remember them?"

Her snippy tone caught me off guard. It didn't sound like her at all. "Of course I remember. I always ask about them, don't I?"

"Well, they're not doing so great. Jade's grades are dropping. She's just decided she doesn't want to eat dinner with her family anymore. And Leah, being the impressionable six-year-old that she is, just follows in her sister's footsteps. Do you know what Eric and I have to go through every night just to get them to sit down at the fucking dinner table?"

I physically drew back at the last sentence. My sister never cursed. The only time I remembered her ever dropping an f-bomb was when she learned the word for the first time as a young child.

"I'm sorry," I said weakly. "Maybe if I come and visit—"

"Forget it. We both know that isn't happening. Once you leave, you make a point to never come back."

A surge of anger flashed inside me. "So we're just going to completely forget that the last two months even happened? I did it. I paid my stupid tribute to my hometown. But I don't belong there. I never did."

"It's sad, Bailey. All those country songs you listen to about never forgetting where you come from, and you shun your own town. You should be ashamed of yourself."

Tears welled up in my eyes as her words sank in deep. They reminded me of what Callie had told me about being a poser. Maybe that was why I'd turned my back on country music when I wrote my new song. It had become a dress that no longer fit me, and I knew it just as well as my sister.

"Well, my fans would agree with you."

She paused. "What do you mean?"

"My new single flopped, to put it mildly. I tried something totally different, and... Let's just say it did not pay off."

"Different how?"

"It has more of a grungy rock sound. I was just going to go for something a little edgier at first, but then my boss came in the studio and had a little talk with me. She thought my song would resonate with people more if I went full-on rock. Clearly,

190

she was way off."

Cassidy was quiet for a beat. "Is this the same boss who threw a hissy fit about you performing at the summer concert?"

"If that's how you want to put it."

She sighed. "You walked right into her trap, Bailey. She *wanted* to see you fail. Don't you get it?"

Like a full-color image on a television screen, I saw the satisfied smile on Lauren's face as she watched me record my song. Now that I was seeing it against the backdrop of my sister's words, it took on a whole new meaning. It had been easy to believe she was on my side after she'd opened up to me about losing out on her dream. Now, I knew that was exactly what she wanted me to think.

"I'm an idiot," I muttered.

"I'm not going to lie. You've always been a little naïve."

I started to respond, but a familiar voice in the background said something I couldn't decipher. Cassidy let out an exasperated sigh. "Not now, Jade. We'll talk about this later."

The voice was clearer and more insistent now. "Why can't you just listen to me? You never listen!"

"I *am* listening. You know I always listen. Now's just not a great time."

"You always say that!"

"Let me talk to her," I said.

Cassidy hesitated for a second before relenting. "Well, you do seem to be the Jade whisperer, so have at it, I guess."

I waited while she passed the phone to her daughter. "Aunt Bailey?" she said in a small voice.

"It's me, sweetie. What's going on?"

All at once, she burst into tears, unleashing a guttural sob that seemed to crawl out of a dark part of her. In between gasps of air, she said, "I don't have any friends anymore. No one wants to sit with me at lunch. Everyone I used to hang out with last year doesn't care about me anymore." She sniffled. "I want to go back to seventh grade."

The similarities between us were more striking than ever. Our first, knee-jerk reaction to facing difficulty in life was to long for a different time. An easier time. My heart went out to her as I recognized how she must be feeling.

"I'm so sorry, honey. I know middle school can be brutal. Trust me, we've all been there."

"Really?"

I chuckled. "Yes, really. I know you can't imagine it at my age, but I was once in eighth grade just like you. And I'm living proof that you *will* survive it."

She sniffled again. "Doesn't seem like it right now."

"Believe me, you will. And then you'll look back at this one day and it won't seem nearly as bad as it does now."

"I guess so."

An idea planted itself inside me, and I felt the corners of my lips turn up into a smile. "Hey, I've got an idea. Why don't I take you to an Electric Ashes concert? They're still on tour, and you seem like you need to blow off some steam. My treat."

I heard her breath catch in her throat. "Seriously? But my mom—"

"Your mom knows you're going through a lot. I know it doesn't seem like it, but she feels your pain. I'm sure she'd be okay with you having fun for one night. And if she isn't, I'll talk to her about it."

"You're the best, Aunt Bailey!" She was practically breathless with excitement. "I can't wait to tell everyone at school. They'll wish they weren't so mean to me when they find out I have

Electric Ashes tickets."

I smiled. "I'll bet. I'll go look at their tour dates right now. I think they're playing a show in Philly next weekend."

"I don't care if they're playing in California. I'll be there."

There was a pause as she passed the phone back to Cassidy. "That's it, huh?" she said, her tone much lighter than it was a few moments ago. "A promise of a concert, and she's a brand-new person."

"Sound like someone you know?" I teased.

"I swear, sometimes I think you should have been her mom instead."

"Life can be funny like that." I smiled. "So, are you okay with her going? Because you didn't seem too happy about it the first time she asked you."

"I'm not the Wicked Witch of the West, you know. I can see that she's hurting. There's a big difference between needing to be disciplined because you're acting like a spoiled brat and actually going through a rough time."

"I'm glad you see that."

"Obviously." She grew quiet all of a sudden. "I'm sorry about your new song. If it makes you feel any better, Jade seems to love it."

That made a smile come to my face, despite all the negative attention my song had attracted. "Well, it is right up her alley."

"You know, I think it was the song she needed right now. It's a good release for all that pent-up stress she has."

"I'm really glad it's helping her. Kind of softens the blow I've had today."

"You'll get through it. You always do."

I gave a small smile. "I know."

After we said goodbye, I headed out to the driveway and got

into my car. I needed to get some air, maybe pick up some groceries. I'd already spent too much time at home obsessing over the success of my song. Time to actually go out and live my life.

I turned onto Main Street and flipped on the radio. Luke Combs's new song was just finishing up. "That was 'Doin' This' by the one and only Luke Combs," the DJ cut in. "I'm DJ Cliff here on WDRX, Pennsylvania's number one country station. I'm taking requests all afternoon, so call in now if you want to hear your favorite. I've got our very first caller right here. What's your name?"

"Dustin, sir."

I gasped, feeling my heart slam against my ribs. *Maybe it's another Dustin,* I thought. But I was only fooling myself. I would know that voice anywhere.

"Where are you calling from, Dustin?"

"Oak Plains."

I could practically hear my heartbeat now. *Oak Plains.* He wasn't in Georgia anymore. He was back home.

"And what song do you want to hear right now?"

"'You Make it Easy' by Jason Aldean. I, uh, have a message for someone, too, if that's all right."

Our song. The one we'd danced to where my old house used to be. An ache bloomed in my chest as the memory swam through my mind.

"Sounds good. I'm sure they'd love to hear it."

I pulled into the parking lot of a strip mall off Main Street and cut the engine, waiting. My breaths were short and shallow as I listened to him.

"I came back for you, baby. I know I've messed up, but I want you to know that I never gave up on us. I miss your smile, the sound of your voice, the sound of your laugh. I'll shout it from the rooftops if I have to. I don't know who I am without you. And I'd do anything to see you standin' there on my doorstep again."

There was a stretched-out pause after he finished. Finally, the DJ gave a low whistle. "Wow. There's one lucky girl out there somewhere. But whoever she is, I don't know how she couldn't take you back after all that." He chuckled. "Anyway, here's 'You Make it Easy' for all you lovebirds out there."

I tore my gaze away from the radio and shifted it toward my phone, which was on silent mode. Only then did I notice the text Dustin had sent two minutes ago. *Turn on the radio,* he'd written. *Your favorite station.*

I shut off the radio and sat in silence, focusing on the rhythm of my breathing. He was back. If I drove to Oak Plains right now and knocked on his door, he would be standing there on the threshold. I would be able to see his smile again. I would be able to touch his face again, to bury myself in his warmth as he held me close. None of it seemed real. Until I saw him in person, I couldn't fully believe he was here.

His message to me played on an endless loop in my mind. *I want you to know that I never gave up on us. I'll shout it from the rooftops if I have to. I don't know who I am without you.* In those words, there was no trace of the man who'd left so suddenly that night. He'd sounded like Dustin again. It was almost as if that night had never happened.

My heart was pulling me in two directions. My body and soul reached out for him while my brain reminded me that I was about to go down a dangerous road. That I should proceed with caution. But my sister's voice still lurked somewhere in my mind, and it was telling me that wasn't how love worked.

Lukewarm didn't cut it. If I wanted him back, I needed to welcome him into my life without a moment's hesitation. And if I didn't, I owed it to him to tell him that.

She was right. I couldn't string him along anymore. Despite what he'd done in the past, he'd made it clear what he wanted now. It was my job now to tell him what I wanted.

And I wanted him. I wanted him more than my own mind could comprehend. But at what cost?

I closed my eyes and rested my head on the seat. Imagining our reunion made me almost weak with joy. But how long would it last? How long before another disappointment snuffed out that joy, making me wish I hadn't been so reckless about guarding it? There were no clear answers. And I wasn't sure whether I wanted to risk finding them out for myself.

I put the car in drive and turned back onto Main Street, letting the familiar storefronts roll past me. Despite all the years I'd lived in Ackerdale, there was a cold, impersonal feeling to the town that I'd never noticed until now. As much as I didn't want to admit it, Oak Plains was nothing like that. Home was embedded in its winding roads, in its forests and fields, and in its caring, big-hearted people. I could go all the way to the ends of the earth, but that simple fact would never change.

A deep sadness tugged at my heart as I stared out the windshield. What was I still doing here? My sister needed me. Jade and Leah needed me. The only friend I had here was Jackie, and considering she had never bothered to text me the whole time I was gone, her status as a friend was questionable at best.

I turned back in the direction of my house, making a mental list of everything I needed to pack. For a moment, I pushed aside my future with Dustin and focused on what I knew was true.

Chapter 16

And I knew I'd been lying to myself when I said I didn't belong in Oak Plains anymore. I'd let suburbia cloud my judgment, had let it push me to release a song that wasn't me at all. In a way, I was glad my single had failed so spectacularly. It was the wake-up call I needed to realize I was losing touch with who I was.

As I headed to my room and started emptying my closet, I made a mental note to verify with Lauren that I could work remotely while I got settled in Oak Plains again. Even though I had a feeling she would happily cater to my wishes after successfully throwing my song off track, I couldn't think about that right now. My mind was already drifting toward long, hot summer days of the past. Days where every corner of my town was an invitation to explore. Days where I felt as light as a blade of grass, as unencumbered as the birdsong that floated on the breeze every morning. Days where I could just be myself, and that was more than enough.

I glanced at the calendar on my desk: September fourteenth. Summer might have been almost over, but maybe it wasn't too late to be that girl again. Maybe she was waiting for me to give her permission to take up space inside me again, running freely like she did across her sprawling backyard as a child.

I kept that image in my mind as I packed my suitcase. But no matter how much I insisted that I was doing this for myself, I couldn't ignore the timing of the desire inside me that was spreading faster than a forest fire. Because it couldn't be mere coincidence that it had taken hold of me as soon as I found out he was back.

Chapter 17

As we found our seats in the densely packed stadium, Jade was talking a mile a minute. "I still can't believe we're actually seeing the Electric Ashes. Everyone at school is going to be *so* jealous. I need to take tons of pictures. Ooh, I hope they open with 'Tears of Crimson.' That's my favorite song. Well, one of my favorites. It's so hard to choose."

I was starting to regret my decision to let her indulge in the lethal combination of soda and junk food during the drive here. Being the fun aunt had its perks, but it was easy to forget why setting boundaries was important too.

"Mine too. Well, it's probably a tie between that and 'Unbreakable.'"

"I love that song!" She grinned at me. "You have awesome taste, Aunt Bailey."

I smiled as we turned our attention to the stage. A metal band that even I'd never heard of was the opening act. While I listened to them screech into their microphones, my thoughts wandered over to work and Lauren. I hadn't been sure how my boss would react to my request to work from home again while I settled back in Oak Plains. As it turned out, I couldn't have asked at a better time. Of course she'd been accommodating to my needs. She'd gotten her way. In her eyes, a loss for my music career was a win for her own career. Which apparently was making sure no one got the chance to live out the dream that had died before her eyes.

Before I could let myself dwell on that for too long, I'd been swept up in the love that had surrounded me upon my return the previous week. My first few steps down my street had been shaky, uncertain. My legs had been weighed down by the shame of shedding my hometown like a bad habit. But when I saw the relief in my sister's eyes, the spring in Leah's step, and a rare joy lighting up Jade's face, I knew it didn't matter if I was gone two months or two years. That would never make my home any less of a home.

Cassidy's house had only been the first stop on my homecoming tour though. After I'd swung by the farm to say hi to Anna, she hadn't even blinked before firing off question after question about Dustin. News of his return had already made the rounds multiple times over. Now, the gossip mill was thirsty for updates on our relationship. That sobering moment had made me face the fact that nothing was sorted out yet. Not until I figured out where I wanted to go next with him.

Jade turned to me now, smiling. "I'm glad you came back."

I smiled back at her. "You know I'm always here for you, right? Even if I'm not physically here. I'm just a phone call away."

Her gaze paused on my face, as if she was about to ask me

something, but the lights went down before she had the chance. The space shook with the collective screams of sixty thousand people as the band members made their dramatic entrance. I hadn't been to an Electric Ashes show since I was a teenager, but I still remembered the way they commanded the stage. I surprised myself by screaming with the same enthusiasm as my niece. I'd forgotten about how good it felt to lose myself in the music instead of the inner world that weighed down my thoughts. The original plan had been to buoy Jade's spirits, but maybe I'd unwittingly given myself the boost I needed too.

I glanced over at my niece, who was beaming like a child on Christmas morning. Her grin shone a light on the rest of her face, and I couldn't help but mirror it. It never failed to amaze me how the power of music could touch another person. She was almost unrecognizable from the brooding teenager my sister faced every day.

I knew that, as her mother, Cassidy would be even more grateful for her daughter's sunnier mood. After the first song ended, I leaned over and said, "Want to take a picture for your mom?"

To my surprise, she smiled and nodded. I angled my phone toward us and snapped a picture. I sent it to my sister with the caption: *Yes, this is your daughter.* Her reply came less than a minute later: *If I knew a concert would get her to smile like that, I would've taken her a long time ago. I owe you one.*

I sent a smiling emoji back just as the next song began. Jade grabbed my arm. "They're playing 'Unbreakable!'"

I threw myself into the energy of the crowd as my favorite song rang out through the stadium. Every song after that was just as electrifying, keeping the audience on its feet up until the very last encore. When the show came to its inevitable close, I felt a pang of disappointment that was reflected in Jade's expression. But I took comfort in knowing that was a sign we'd both had an incredible time.

We followed the mass of fans out of the stadium while Jade scrolled through all the photos she'd taken during the show. "I need to post these right away. I can't wait to see the look on Alexis's face when she sees them."

"I'm glad you had fun." I spied my car in the parking lot and led Jade toward it. "Now let's get you home before your mom starts to worry."

After we piled into the car, I sent a quick text to Cassidy to let her know we were on our way back. The venue in Philly was a little under three hours away from Oak Plains, and it was late enough that traffic wouldn't be an issue. Still, I knew if Jade stepped into my sister's house a minute after the promised time of eleven thirty, I wouldn't hear the end of it.

Three hours later, I made a right on Acorn Lane and pulled in front of Cassidy's house. My sister came to the door before I had the chance to knock, a telltale sign that she'd been watching out for us from the window.

Cassidy made a show of checking her watch. "You barely made it."

"And yet your daughter is in one piece. I'd say that's cause for celebration."

Jade snorted, earning her a stern look from her mother. "You've been hanging around Aunt Bailey for too long. Time to get ready for bed, missy."

Jade responded with an eye roll before saving her brightest smile for me. "Thanks, Aunt Bailey. I had the best night ever."

She locked me into a tight hug, her head buried in my chest. I surprised myself by fighting back tears. Ever since I moved to Ackerdale, I'd been happy with paying the occasional visit to my hometown to see my nieces. But after having spent the entire summer with them, a stronger, more durable bond now held us together. I needed them, I supposed, just as much as they needed me.

After Jade and I had exchanged goodbyes, I smiled at Cassidy. "I would say hi to Leah, too, but I'm guessing she's sound asleep by now."

"She is. But you know you can stop by whenever you want, especially since you're so close."

Now that I was staying in Oak Plains for the foreseeable future, I'd opted to rent a small cottage next to the bed-and-breakfast down the street. It was a simple, sparsely decorated space, stripped of any personality. It was eerily reminiscent of my current situation. Even though I was confident in my decision to come home, I felt like I was floating aimlessly through town, a leaf swirling in the wind with nowhere to land. Every time I wondered where I would go next, my thoughts crept back to Dustin and what he'd said on the radio. And then I remembered that the next move was entirely mine.

As if reading my mind, Cassidy said, "So, you're still not speaking to Dustin after he poured his heart out to you?"

I pressed my lips together. "I can't make myself that vulnerable again."

"Love is all about vulnerability, Bailey. He knows that better than you. Didn't you hear him express his deepest feelings on the radio? And for the whole state to hear. He didn't just do that to embarrass himself. He did that because you're worth it to him." She held her gaze on me. "But apparently he's not worth it to you."

The words sliced deep, just as she'd probably intended. "Cass,"

I said in a small, wounded voice. "How can you say that when you know what I've been through?"

"We've all been through stuff. The difference is that some people choose not to let it define them."

"Don't you think I want to be with him more than anything? Why do you think I came all the way back here?"

She gave me a long, hard look. "Until you knock on his door and tell him you forgive him, nothing you're saying has any weight."

I knew she was right. That was the worst part. I swallowed. "Well, thanks for letting me take Jade to the concert. We both had a great time."

With that, I turned and walked over to my car. I started the engine and drove off without knowing where I planned to go. I was too restless to go home, but Oak Plains was a ghost town at this hour. My only two options were the convenience store and the twenty-four-hour gas station.

Before I could make a decision, I found myself turning into the convenience store parking lot. I got out of the car and decided that a quick walk past the shelves would help clear my thoughts. I walked into the store and idly browsed the selections of food, toiletries, and magazines. I was so absorbed in my surroundings that I almost didn't hear the conversation at the register.

"So, you're new to town?"

I whipped my head around to spot the cashier talking to a young woman standing by the register. She had a shopping cart parked next to her filled with baby essentials. Newcomers were rare enough in Oak Plains, but someone so young with her whole life ahead of her was even rarer. What could she possibly be looking for in a little town like ours?

"My aunt lives here, so we're familiar with the area," the woman said. "My husband and I have recently started looking for a new home here. There's so much potential from what we've seen so far, and we both think it's the perfect place to raise our Catherine."

The cashier started scanning her items. "Got your eye on anything yet?"

"We were driving down Acorn Lane earlier today, and we saw this huge yard with a mailbox but no house. It looked like there used to be a house there that got torn down or something. We asked one of the neighbors about it, and she said the whole house burned to the ground a few years ago. Which is a shame. But it makes me wonder why no one has rebuilt all this time."

I stood there frozen the whole time she spoke. I hadn't heard anyone even mention my old house in years. The cashier caught my eye, and she held her gaze on me. Unlike the newcomer, she knew the full story behind that empty yard. Everyone in Oak Plains did. And they knew that I still hadn't released those ashes from my grasp.

"Anyway, my husband and I want to do something about that big yard. It's a great location, not too far from the school, and the neighbors are so friendly. So, we decided we're going to see if we can buy it and build a new house. We're going to hire an architect and builders. Plus, it won't hurt that my husband is pretty handy himself." Her smile was exuberant. "We can't wait to see what we can do with it."

Her plan shouldn't have felt like a slap in the face, but it did. It was only natural for a new family to want to occupy the space my family and I once had. Life moved forward. But as I watched the woman chatter away about her big plans, it struck me that I wasn't moving forward with life. I was standing still while the scenery blurred past me. I was letting the past play on repeat until it obliterated both my present and my future. Until there was nothing left for me to hold onto.

The cashier pursed her lips and gave me a sideways glance. "I think there's someone you should talk to first."

Following her gaze, the woman turned and faced me. She seemed to look past me at first, like she wasn't sure if I was the right person. When her eyes finally settled on me, she said, "Do I know you?"

My mouth dried up as I searched for an explanation. "That used to be my house. The one that burned down." I took a shaky breath. "My parents still own that plot of land. It holds a lot of sentimental value for all of us, which is why they haven't sold it yet. You would have to speak to them first if you're thinking about buying the land."

She looked a little taken aback, like she couldn't understand why someone would hold on to a barren piece of land for six years. I suddenly felt ridiculous for saying anything, and I wished the cashier hadn't set up our exchange. But anyone who'd lived in this town for more than six years knew what that place meant to my family and me. She'd only said something out of the kindness of her heart.

The woman met my eyes. Her surprise had begun to melt away from her features, making room for empathy. "Well, I would really appreciate it if you'd arrange for us to meet with your parents. We really want to take this next step, but we wouldn't feel right doing it if you're still emotionally invested in the area."

My eyes flicked over to the cart of baby supplies next to her. I thought of the new family she was starting and how excited she was to begin the next chapter in her life. She had something to look forward to. A goal to strive toward. And here I was, holding her back. Forcing her to hit pause on her life while I tried to figure out my own. She didn't deserve that. She deserved to go after her dreams, full speed ahead, without anyone stopping her.

I forced a smile. "Of course. I'll give them a call. It's a lovely area, and I think you and your husband would love it." I swallowed the lump in my throat. "And when she grows up, your daughter will realize how lucky she was to grow up in such a beautiful town."

She must have heard the catch in my voice, because there was a hint of sadness in her eyes when she smiled. "Thank you. That means the world to both of us." She started to turn her head, but then faced me again. "I'm sorry. I didn't get your name."

I told her, and she smiled warmly. "I'm Miranda." She gave me her number and slipped her phone back into her purse. "We'll keep in touch."

I nodded while the cashier handed her a receipt. Miranda gave a little wave and headed out of the store. I stood there dumbly for a minute before slinging my bag over my shoulder and finding my way toward the parking lot. Once I was inside my car, I lay my head back against the seat and replayed that scene in my mind. Hearing Miranda talk about my old house had triggered something inside me that I hadn't known existed. More importantly, it had showed me that I still wasn't over that period in my life, no matter what I tried to tell myself. I hadn't properly healed from the pain after it happened. Instead, I'd run off to Ackerdale, burying my feelings along with all of my bad memories. And now I was paying the price.

If I ever wanted to be truly happy in this town—the full kind of happiness that I missed to my core—I would need to get past the roadblock that was keeping me from getting there. And that was the day we lost our home. The day I lost a part of who I was.

Everything went back to that one night. And it was about time I started working through that piece of my past before I faced my future.

Chapter 18

As we walked out of the recording studio together a few days later, Madison was still grinning from ear to ear. She'd barely been able to squeeze out her lyrics during the recording session, she was so excited. Even though I was happy for her, it hurt a little to watch her. She seemed to be getting closer to finding her sound every day while I grew further and further from mine.

I studied her for a moment as she tapped out a text on her phone. It was hard to believe I was looking at the same girl who'd forgotten the lyrics in front of everyone at the Violet Hearts concert. The Madison I knew now carried herself with a quiet confidence—the look of a woman who was comfortable in her own skin. Knowing I'd helped mold her into that person should have filled me with pride, but instead it made me inexplicably sad. Maybe it was because I'd always pictured us sharing the same confidence, not her rising to the top while

I only got kicked down lower and lower.

"How do you do that?" I asked.

She looked up from her phone. "Do what?"

"Stay so excited about singing all the time." I realized how pathetic that must have sounded coming from a singer, and I sighed. "I guess I've been in a rut for a pretty long time now. I mean, I *was* excited when I wrote some new songs over the summer, but that just seems like a fluke now."

She considered me. "Do you know how I came up with the idea for the song I just recorded?"

I shook my head.

"I was sitting at home a few months ago, feeling kind of lonely, when I started thinking about my brother. We were never that close growing up. As soon as he turned eighteen, he left Hayestown and moved all the way to San Francisco. We didn't talk much over the years. But that day, I decided I wanted to change that. So I booked a plane ticket and flew over to visit him. I wasn't sure how he would react, but it turned out he was feeling lonely too. Now we talk all the time, and it's all because I chose to do something about it."

She looked at me. "My point is, if you want to get excited about singing again, you need to do something worth singing about."

I let her words sink in. When I glanced over at her, I shook my head and started to laugh.

She furrowed her brow. "What's so funny?"

I gestured to the two of us. "Don't you see how our roles have completely reversed? You're the mentor now. Now that I think about it, you probably give me better advice than I ever gave you."

She thought about what I said, and then she was laughing too.

"You have a point. But hey, don't sell yourself short. There's no way I would've taken on that crowd at the summer concert if it weren't for your coaching."

I smiled gratefully. Surveying the parking lot, I spotted my car at the far end. "Well, I'd better go find something worth singing about, then." I stopped and looked at her again. "Oh, and great job in the studio today. I can tell that song came straight from the heart."

"It did. And I'm sure you have plenty of songs like that waiting inside you."

I turned over Madison's advice in my mind during the three-hour drive home. *Do something worth singing about.* It was good advice, if only I could find something interesting enough to turn into a song. Besides, my feelings were still tangled up in Miranda's unexpected news and Dustin's public plea for me to come back to him. I needed to sort through everything that had happened this past week before I worried about finding inspiration for new music.

I drove down Acorn Lane and approached Cassidy's house, which was only a few houses away from the cottage I was renting. On a whim, I turned onto her driveway and parked beside her car. The story Madison had shared about her brother made me want to pay a quick visit to my sister. Even though we'd always been close, unlike Madison and her brother, Madison's story was the reminder I needed that it was never a bad idea to carve out time for family.

After I rang the bell, Eric came to the door instead of Cassidy. He smiled. "Good to see you, Bailey. I was just in the backyard with Leah. You can come out and join us if you want."

Knowing Leah would be happy to see me, I nodded. "I'd love to."

The air seemed colder in the backyard now that fall was edging its way in. The last time I'd been here, it was still the heart of summertime. Being in the same place after the air had been stripped of its warmth gave the atmosphere a cold, eerie feel. A sudden chill curled its icy fingers around my body, making me shiver. It felt like summer itself turning its back on me.

"Where's Leah?" I asked Eric.

He pointed to the tree house. "She must have escaped there while I was gone. It's been her favorite place in the world since we finished renovating it." He stepped closer to the small wooden house and called, "Leah, come say hi to Aunt Bailey!"

You mean since Dustin finished renovating it, I corrected him silently. I wasn't sure why I felt such a strong need to credit Dustin when we still weren't on speaking terms. Maybe it was because I was standing right in front of the tree house where we'd shared our first kiss that summer. As I remembered the tender way he'd cupped my face in his hands, the way he'd tasted me like he couldn't believe I was really his, I felt my throat constrict. I'd worked so hard trying to protect myself from my own feelings that I hadn't let myself miss him. But I did miss him. I'd missed him since the minute he told me he was leaving. And now that I'd set those feelings free, there was no way to fold them up and stuff them back inside me.

"Aunt Bailey!" Leah scampered down the steps and wrapped her arms around me. For a moment, I set my messy thoughts aside and gave my attention to my niece.

"Hey there, buttercup." I knelt down and tousled her hair. "You having fun in the tree house?"

"It's the best. Mr. Cooper rocks!"

I swallowed thickly. "Yes, he does."

"He even built a toy chest just for me. You wanna see?"

He built her a toy chest? It took me a second to collect myself, but when I did, I tried my best to force an eager smile. "I'd love to."

She hurried back up the stairs while I followed. When I glimpsed the inside of the tree house, I did a double take. The space was unrecognizable from the last time I'd been in it with Dustin. What used to be a bare, minimalist room peppered with haphazardly placed toys had been transformed into a verifiable playroom. Plush beanbag chairs encircled a lava lamp that sat on a side table showcasing a stack of children's books. The walls boasted a display of what looked like Leah's drawings from art class. In the far corner was my treasured dollhouse from childhood, the one Cassidy had handed down to her two daughters. Now that Jade had outgrown it, I could see that her sister had happily taken ownership of the toy.

I couldn't help but feel a pang of jealousy as I looked around me. I would have given anything for a room like this when I was Leah's age.

"Come see!" Leah led me to a far corner of the room, where a sturdy wooden chest sat against the wall. It was painted bright green—Leah's favorite color—and had her initials emblazoned in white. She opened the chest to reveal dozens of toys piled on top of each other. "Isn't it perfect?" she asked, beaming.

I tried to respond, but I was too entranced by the creation in front of me. I ran a finger across the sleek wood, thinking, *He made this. He did this all for Leah—and not because he had to. Because he wanted to.*

I thought back to when Leah had interrupted us while we were kissing up here. Dustin had been so warm toward my niece, and he'd said all the right things to her. That memory, coupled with the gift he'd given her, said far more about the kind of man he was than his radio message ever did.

When I climbed down the stairs to the lawn, Cassidy was in the middle of a conversation with Eric. She stopped talking as soon as she saw me, as if she knew what I was going to say.

"He made that for her," I said, pointing to the tree house. "He built that entire toy chest just for her."

"Yes, he did, Bailey," she said softly. Just from hearing her tone, I knew she shared all the thoughts about Dustin that were running through my head.

I felt a drop of rain land on my skin, followed by several others. Cassidy looked up at the sky and placed a hand on Leah's back. "It's starting to rain. Time to head inside."

She ushered her daughter into the house while I stood on the dampening lawn, letting the rain fall freely onto my face. My thoughts wandered until they landed on Miranda and her rebuilding project. My parents had happily agreed to sell the land when I spoke to them on the phone after meeting Miranda at the store. They'd assured me that if I was ready to hand over the land to another family, they wouldn't hesitate to send over the paperwork. Miranda and her husband had already filled out all the documents, which meant they were free to embark on their home-building journey. Miranda had seemed nothing short of eager to get started, so I wouldn't be surprised if she and her husband had already rounded up a crew of workers to start clearing the land.

The thought of the rebuilding going on without me planted a strange feeling of loneliness inside me. It might not have been my home anymore, but it would always live inside my heart. Besides, Miranda herself had invited me to stop by whenever I wanted when we spoke on the phone. As painful as it would be to witness a new home staking its claim on the grassy carpet of my childhood, it felt like something I needed to be a part of.

Before I could decide what I was doing, I got into my car and started driving down our street. I needed to shelve this chapter of my past once and for all. It was the only way I could move forward to the present, where Dustin was patiently waiting for me. And the first step was going right to the scene of the crime.

* * *

As I approached the site of my old house, I realized I hadn't planned out what I would say to Miranda and her husband if they were there. I hadn't thought anything through before coming here. I'd just felt a pull that had brought me here—the same pull that had led me to drive to the hardware store the second time I saw Dustin. It came from somewhere deeper than myself, giving me no choice but to follow it.

I parked right in front of the mailbox, remembering when Dustin had brought me here. He'd been right when he said I would think of us dancing together whenever I drove past my old front lawn. But instead of being relieved that I had a new, happy memory to replace the old one, I felt a cavernous void inside me where Dustin used to be. The all-encompassing hollowness of it was even worse than the sadness the fire had left behind.

I got out of the car and made my way up the driveway. The rain had let up, but the dark-gray blanket above me held a warning of more to come. When I rounded the corner, I spotted Miranda pacing back and forth on the lawn, wringing her hands as she spoke. A tall, lanky man that I guessed was her husband stood beside her, attempting to console her. Just a cursory glance at their body language told me something was very wrong.

I walked up to them hesitantly, feeling like I was overstepping an invisible boundary. I'd been expecting to see them celebrating their new project, maybe blasting their favorite music on a portable speaker while planning out their future home together. Even though it would have hurt more to see that, it was what I should have seen. Not the two of them looking like they'd already regretted the whole ordeal.

The thought hit me right in the sternum. *Did* they regret it?

"Hi, guys," I said with a little wave. I looked over at the man and extended my hand to him. "I'm Bailey. I met Miranda at the convenience store a few days ago, and she told me about her plan to build a new home. I used to live in the old house here. I think it's wonderful that you're giving this place another chance."

He shook my hand and smiled. "Nice to meet you, Bailey. Miranda told me about you. I'm Wes, her husband."

Miranda offered up a weary smile. "I wish you'd come by after we made some progress. Our entire land-clearing team canceled on us. They ate some sketchy takeout while they were working on another project, and they all came down with food poisoning." She turned around and grimaced at the yellowed grass behind us. "So now we're still stuck at square one."

I sucked in air between my teeth. "I'm sorry to hear that. But I'm sure things will straighten out soon."

Miranda buried her face in her hands. "First the flood, now this."

I looked at Wes. "What flood?"

"We're staying at her aunt's while we build our new house," he explained. "We woke up to find her whole bathroom flooded.

One of the pipes must've burst. I shut off the water and had a look at it, but I'm at a loss for what to do."

"Apparently, neither of us is as handy as we thought. We don't know where we're supposed to find a plumber around here." Miranda looked skyward. "Besides, it looks like we're in for a downpour. Who's going to bother coming out here now?"

My heart knew the answer before I did. *Neither of us is as handy as we thought,* she'd said. But I knew someone who was. Someone who'd breathed new life into Leah's beloved tree house. Someone who'd built a whole chest of toys from scratch out of the goodness of his heart. Someone who wouldn't blink at the thought of getting his hands dirty or breaking a sweat. Especially when the goal was to help someone else.

My first instinct was to call him and tell him what was going on. But after all the hurdles and miscommunication we'd dealt with, a phone call felt inadequate. We needed to see each other face-to-face.

I looked at Miranda. "Actually, I have someone in mind. A family friend who also happens to be a handyman. I'm sure he could take a look."

It was like someone had lit a lantern from within her. With a radiant smile, she said, "You're a lifesaver. Can you get him to come over now?"

I thought for a second. "How about I run out to the hardware store real quick? He also works shifts there, and he's probably at the store now. I'll make sure he has all the tools you need before he stops by. Where does your aunt live?"

"18 Marigold Drive."

"We'll meet you over there."

Miranda nodded eagerly as I returned to my car and started the engine. My heart wouldn't quit thumping during the entire drive. It had been easy to promise to talk to Dustin under the guise of helping out a friend. But now that I was getting closer and closer to the store, reality was sinking in. And the reality was that I still had no idea where we stood or how he would react to seeing me again. Or, better yet, how I would react to seeing *him*.

After pulling into the Cooper Hardware lot, I slowly got out of the car. I entered the store like a shoplifter, my eyes darting wildly from side to side. I wove my way through every aisle in search of him. After circling the entire store twice, I came up empty-handed. There was no trace of him anywhere.

I walked up to the register, where Dustin's friend Ron was scrolling through his phone. "Hey, Ron. Any chance you've seen Dustin?"

He looked up from his phone with a shrug. "Don't think so. Haven't been seeing a lot of him lately, to be honest. He's been real quiet since he got back from Georgia."

I tried to smile. "Well, thanks anyway." While I turned toward the exit, I decided it was best if I called Dustin. I couldn't keep dancing delicately around what needed to be done. Besides, I wasn't just doing this for Miranda and Wes anymore. The more imminent his presence became, the more I could feel him in the air around me. And the more I wondered how I went without him for so long. It was like I'd filtered all the oxygen out of the air for the past few weeks, and now I realized I hadn't been breathing all this time.

I stepped back into the lot and started heading to my car. I had my fingers curled around the door handle when I heard a familiar voice drifting from behind the store.

I whirled around and walked slowly toward the source of the voice. It took me a few moments to figure out that he was singing. I moved closer until I could make out the words.

You think you have it all
    Until one day, you don't.
    You hold on tight to all the good times
    Until you have no choice but to let go.

I stood there, my breath trapped in my lungs. He was singing my song to himself. And not just any song. It was "Bitter," the one that had bombed magnificently.

I'd written that song to express all the pent-up feelings I had about him. Now he was singing it absently to himself, echoing the lyrics right back to me. It hit me that he probably interpreted the words in a whole different way. *I* was the good times he'd had, and I'd given him no choice but to let go of them.

Until now.

I rounded the corner of the store and saw him unloading a new shipment that had arrived. His baseball cap was pulled down low over his eyes, just like the first time I saw him at the store. He didn't notice me standing there. I couldn't tell if he was simply distracted or if he chose not to see me.

I took a deep breath and, so softly I barely heard myself, said, "And then, one day, she comes back."

He looked up and met my eyes for the first time in what felt like a century. I'd never seen him so still before. He beheld the sight of me without so much as breathing, as if he were afraid the slightest movement would make me disappear. Like fighting wakefulness at the end of a beautiful dream.

He took a step toward me, and I noticed his eyes were glistening with tears. He gently brushed his fingers across my face. "It's really you, isn't it?"

I smiled. "The only Bailey Flynn in town."

He smiled, and it was like sunlight dousing the entire countryside. I wanted to wrap my arms around him and bury my head in his chest, breathing in the smell of him that had become as familiar to me as my own skin. But there was too much to sort through first. And I couldn't forget the reason I'd come here to begin with.

I looked at him steadily. "We have a lot to talk about. But first, we need to head over to Marigold Drive and help someone." I told him about selling the land to Miranda and the predicament she and Wes were in.

A small smile crept onto his face. "Well, I never thought I'd see the day Bailey Flynn let go of 245 Acorn Lane for good. I'm proud of you, you know. And I'd be happy to help these folks out. Wouldn't be the first pipe I've had to fix." He turned toward his truck. "Let me just grab my tools."

Once he had everything he needed, we piled into my car. I took the wheel as we made our way to Miranda's aunt's house. He was quiet beside me the whole time I drove. I ached to know what he was thinking, but this wasn't the time or place. I could sense that he was wondering the same of me. How did we get to the point where simple communication was out of reach?

I found the mailbox bearing the number 18 and parked in front of it. We jumped out of the car to find Miranda waiting for us on the lawn. She smiled at Dustin. "You must be the handyman Bailey was talking about."

"Yes, ma'am." Dustin tipped his hat. "Dustin Cooper, at your service."

She turned toward the house. "Okay, let's get started. It's supposed to start raining at six, so I don't want you to get caught in it."

Wes was waiting for us in the house. Dustin followed the couple up the stairs to the bathroom while I waited in the foyer. As he worked, he patiently explained what had gone wrong and what he needed to do to fix it. Even though I only caught a few words here and there, I could tell he was doing more than simply repairing the pipe. He was taking his time to help her understand the job ahead. He taught her in the same way he taught me to fish at the creek—not in a condescending or rushed tone but in a clear way that allowed the student to grasp every word without being afraid to ask questions.

As I listened, I felt the gravity of what I'd almost lost. The first man in my life who'd wanted me for who I really was. Who'd walked alongside me as I healed from my trauma. Who'd never rushed me as I tried to find my footing again. I knew deep inside me that what he'd done that night wasn't out of a desire to hurt me. Maybe I didn't know his reasons yet, but I saw now how afraid he'd been. Just like I'd been afraid when I left Oak Plains at twenty-two. And if he needed me to walk alongside him as he found his way again, just like he'd done for me, I would be there. I knew I would, with every fiber of my being.

Dustin finished the job in about half an hour. Outside, dense, dark clouds began squeezing out fat drops of rain. Raindrops were pelting the windows when Miranda, Wes, and Dustin reached the foot of the stairs. "Thank you so much for coming by," Miranda said to Dustin. "I think my husband and I are prepared for the next plumbing disaster, now that you explained everything so well."

"Anytime." He nodded at me. "Bailey's got my number, in case you ever need it." He winked at me, making my heart flutter.

Miranda reached for her purse and pulled out her wallet. "How much do I owe you?"

Dustin waved her off. "Y'all don't worry about that now. Just helping out our new neighbors."

She and Wes looked taken aback, like they'd never seen that kind of generosity back where they came from. "Oh, but I couldn't—" Miranda began, but Dustin was already smiling and holding up a hand in a goodbye as he opened the door. "I'll see y'all around town," he said.

The rain had kicked up a notch by the time we reached my car. I hurried inside while Dustin slid into the passenger seat. As I started heading back to the hardware store, I said, "That was really kind of you."

He shrugged. "Just wanted to make them feel welcome."

My throat went dry as I approached the store. The air still felt too thick, our words still too practiced. I was beginning to wonder if we would ever be able to return to the way we'd been before that night.

The rain was coming down harder by the time I pulled into the hardware store lot. I cut the engine and opened my mouth to say something. Only I had no idea what I wanted to say.

"Come in the store," he said. "I wanna show you something."

I peered through the drenched windshield, which made the hardware store look like an abstract watercolor painting. "I should probably head back. This rain isn't letting up anytime soon."

He looked at me with a glimmer in his eye. "Just go with the flow, Bailey."

He'd said the same thing to me while he drove to my old house after we'd reconnected. For some reason, those words had the same effect on me, and I found myself opening the car door without further questions. "Just let me grab my umbrella."

I was reaching into the trunk to fetch the umbrella when I felt his arms around my waist. I turned around, startled. Before I could speak, he took my face in his hands and kissed me. It was the desperate, passionate kiss of two people who thought they'd lost what they had forever. As I stood there, the rain soaking my clothes through and drenching my hair, I realized I didn't need an umbrella anymore.

When we pulled away, I failed to find a single word. He still had my face cupped in his hands, holding it like it was some kind of treasure. He ran his thumbs down my rain-streaked face and whispered, "I'll never let you go again."

My throat constricted. His words reminded me of the night of the summer concert and how I still didn't know why he'd left. "We have a lot to talk about," I said quietly.

He looked down and nodded. He walked into the hardware store with me alongside him. Once we were safely inside the back room, I shut the door and sat next to him. Peering at him closely, I asked, "What happened?"

He didn't speak for a long moment, as if he was carefully gathering his words. The rain pelted the window beside the back door, gobbling up the silence inside the small room. In a low voice, he said, "My sister overdosed the night of the concert."

All the oxygen fled my lungs. I looked up at him, unable to speak. He went on before I had the chance to find words. "Her boyfriend happened to come over that night, and he found her unconscious. He called 911, and they rushed her to the hospital. When I got the call, she wasn't doing well at all."

He paused and looked away, and I let him take the time he needed. Once he'd collected himself, he said, "I flew down there as fast as I could. My dad came along too. The second I saw her, I knew it was bad. This wasn't the first time she's been in the hospital, but I could tell things were much worse this time." He cast his eyes downward. "She managed to hold on until the next day, but…"

Tears gathered in his eyes, and I pulled him close. We sat there in silence, letting our tears fall freely. I felt in my heart that we were both open to baring our scars to one another, no matter how raw they were. And there was no one else in the world we wanted to be with while we healed.

I wiped a tear away from his face. "I'm so sorry. Whatever you need, I'm here. Even if you just need someone to listen."

His eyes were sad as he gave me a small smile. My heart ached for him while I tried to comprehend the amount of pain he was feeling. I couldn't even fathom the same thing happening to Cassidy. Even though Dustin wasn't as close to his sister as I was to mine, what happened to her would leave a scar that wouldn't ever heal completely.

In light of what he'd just told me, his strange behavior the night of the concert made sense now. I held onto his arm. "I shouldn't have pushed you to explain what happened that night. You were in shock. That was selfish of me."

He shook his head. "No, Bailey. I should've told you. Relationships don't work if both people aren't totally honest with each other. Besides, I know what you've been through, and you must've expected the worst. No one can blame you for that."

I looked at him. "I want you to know that I wasn't upset because you left. I was upset because you didn't tell me *why* you were leaving."

"I know." He paused to think for a moment, his mind somewhere else. "You remember Gina, right?"

I nodded. "Your girlfriend in high school."

"She was the first girl I ever really loved. Or, hell, *thought* I loved. I didn't know a damn thing about love when I was seventeen." He gave his head a little shake. "Anyway, things got pretty serious junior year. I took her to prom, and it just kinda hit me that night. She made me happier than anyone else, and I knew she was the one I wanted to be with." He glanced over at me. "You never got to show me how wrong I was."

I managed a weak smile as he went on.

"The weekend after prom night, I invited her over for dinner to meet my dad. All three of my siblings still lived here back then. Times were simpler. But they also weren't.

"Everything went well at first. But then, around eight, Kelsea—my sister—stumbled into the house, already slurring her words. She was trying to quit opioids on her own, but the withdrawal symptoms were too much for her to handle. So she started drinking to cope.

"I trusted Gina, and I really believed she would understand. So I started explaining Kelsea's situation to her. I had to stop halfway through, though, because I saw how afraid she was. I could see in her eyes that she just realized what she'd gotten herself into. It was like she didn't even see me anymore. She just saw all the problems I brought into her life." He lowered his eyes and pressed his lips together. "Right before she was about to leave, all the alcohol Kelsea drank caught up to her, and she threw up all over the kitchen floor. Some of it landed right on Gina's heels. Gina looked horrified. Just before she turned to leave, she looked me straight in the eye and said, 'Don't ever bring a girl home again.'"

He turned to me. "I know it doesn't excuse what I did. But what happened really messed with my head. After that night, I felt so ashamed that I swore I would never let anyone get close to my family. That was the first time I let myself open up to someone, and I regretted it. Gina never spoke another word to me after that."

My heart sank as I took in his words. I shook my head. "That was horrible the way she treated you. She didn't deserve you." My voice softened. "And you don't have to explain anything. I understand. If you'd just told me that from the start, I would've understood then too."

"When I came back into the venue and saw you, I had a flashback to when Gina left me. I wasn't thinking straight. I just thought, *I can't let this happen again.* But I was an idiot for thinking you would react like her. I know you would never do that."

"We both have our own scars that need to heal. I can't say I haven't let the fire hold me back from living my life. But we both need to be transparent with each other from now on. I hope you know that."

"I do know that. I really do." A shadow of a smile found its way onto his face. "Anyway, Gina leaving ended up being the best thing that ever happened to me. If it wasn't for that, I wouldn't be sittin' here with you right now."

I grinned. "You should've known Gina wasn't right for you. I mean, how are you gonna get down in the Georgia clay with a girl who only wears designer shoes?"

To my surprise, he laughed out loud—the belly laugh that I'd come to miss over the past few weeks. When he stopped laughing, he shook his head. "Bailey Flynn, you never fail to surprise me."

"What do you mean?"

"If you'd told me I'd find a reason to laugh again this soon, I don't think I would've believed you."

It seemed like the worst injustice that someone as carefree and fun loving as him could ever be in such a dark place. I nestled into him and rested my head on his shoulder. "You always find a reason to laugh. It's one of the many things I love about you."

We sat like that for a while until something resurfaced in my mind. Something he'd said to me before he left for Georgia. I lifted my head to look at him. "What did you mean when you said you didn't want to ruin my happiness that night?"

Quietly, he said, "I didn't want my pain to become your pain."

I blinked back tears as he continued.

"I remember that song you wrote about wanting a simpler life. The one you said was inspired by your visit to Anna's farm. I knew I couldn't promise you that kind of life, so I…" His voice trailed off.

I looked at him intently. "I don't want any life that doesn't have you in it. You know that, right?"

Relief warmed his face. "I know."

"But we can't have any more secrets, okay? You have to promise me that. Otherwise, this is never going to work."

His eyes grew intense, like he was thinking hard about something. He took my hands in his and steadied his gaze on my face. "Come to Georgia with me."

"What?" I faltered.

"Come with me. I want to show you where I come from. I love you, Bailey, and I can't stand losing you again. If you want there to be no more secrets between us, this is the only way I can show you who I really am."

I couldn't bring myself to speak at first. Finally, I shook my head and chuckled. "Dustin Cooper, you never fail to surprise me."

Chapter 18

"Is that a yes?"

I smiled at him. "I'm still the same girl who asked what it was like in Georgia all those years ago. And I still want to find out."

He laughed and wrapped me in a bear hug. "You'll love it down there. I know it."

I let him stroke my hair while I pressed my face against his chest. "Oh, and one more thing," I said.

He pulled away so he could look at me. "What's that?"

I looked at the man I'd been apart from for much too long. The man I hadn't given the time of day back in high school, only to regret it deeply now. The man I'd been through so much with, even though we'd only truly known each other for a few months. It might have taken me losing touch with who I was to see it, but I knew that I felt more for him than I'd ever felt for another human. He was the only one I envisioned being with through all the dizzying highs and all the soul-crushing lows. And I knew with every cell in my body that he felt the same way too.

You'll know if he doesn't love you, Cassidy had told me once. *There won't be any room for doubt. If you really do trust him, you won't see this as the end.*

It wasn't the end. Far from it. This was the beginning of countless other beginnings we would share together, as long as we were open to them.

"I love you too," I whispered.

And for once in my life, I didn't feel a single trace of doubt.

Chapter 19

⁓⊶⊷⁓

The setting sun hung low over Mapleville, painting the cornfield across Dustin's childhood home a deep golden hue. I stood beside him, admiring the bucolic scenery that reminded me of home. *Kinda like Oak Plains, plus the southern charm,* he'd told me that day in high school. I'd only been here for less than two hours, but I couldn't have chosen a more fitting description.

After reuniting with Dustin, I'd updated Cassidy and Evelyn on my relationship with him. Evelyn had been happy for me in a mature, subdued kind of way. It was Cassidy who hadn't been able to contain her giddiness. Normally, I would have rolled my eyes at her reaction, but I found myself welcoming her unbridled joy now that I felt that way myself.

I remembered what Evelyn told me when we'd run into each other at the Violet Hearts concert at the start of summer. *It wasn't getting your hopes up that made you this way. It was abandoning hope.* Her words rang true with a whole different meaning now. The difference was that now, I wasn't relying on happiness to carry me through. Happiness was a fleeting feeling that was hinged on one's current circumstances. It could dissipate just as quickly as it had appeared. But hope was more robust. It affirmed that things might not be okay right now, but they would be. And harboring that knowledge inside me was more than enough.

I glanced over at Dustin. He looked content, like he couldn't ask for anything more in that moment. And neither could I. We still had a long way to go relationship wise, but for now, we were happy where we were. I could feel that happiness emanate from him as he wrapped an arm around me, taking in the familiar sights of his hometown with the woman he loved.

"You know, you haven't written a new song in a while," he said.

His comment reminded me of Madison's advice to do something worth singing about. Her suggestion had taken a back seat to everything else that had happened over the past few days. Now, though, it sat center stage, reminding me that I had a job to do.

"You know," I said, "someone once told me that the best way to find inspiration for a new song is to do something worth singing about."

"Oh, really? Do you have something in mind?"

"We're on your turf," I said teasingly. "You tell me."

He took a moment to think and let loose a knowing grin. "I know exactly what you need to do. It's still hot enough to go down to Sycamore Point."

"Where's that?"

"You'll see. Believe me, you won't be disappointed."

I shrugged and went back into the house, where I slipped off my high-heeled sandals in favor of something more comfortable. I scoured the contents of my suitcase, but I couldn't find the sneakers I'd packed. "Hold on. I can't find my shoes."

He laughed. "You won't be needing shoes, Bailey."

My confusion only grew as I followed him into his truck. Once we started moving, he rolled down the window and turned up a Garth Brooks song he'd cued up on his phone. He let out a loud whoop. "Welcome to Georgia," he said, laying on the drawl extra thick.

I laughed at his silliness, but I'd never felt more at home than I did in that moment. Statuesque pines kept watch over us, and every twist and turn held a new treasure—whether it was a white-tailed deer peeking out from behind a tree or a cluster of azaleas smiling at us from the side of the road. Even though the sun was on its way out, the heat barely abated in its intensity. The South Georgia heat in September was comparable to Pennsylvania weather in late July.

When we pulled up to Sycamore Point a little under an hour later, the natural beauty surrounding us physically stole my breath. Thick, imposing sycamore trees—the namesake of the street—shot up into the sky, practically swooping in to replace the tall, thin pines that had surrounded us just moments ago. Stars were beginning to dot the ink-black sky, which seemed impressively larger than it did back home. Sitting at the heart of it all was a long, meandering creek, its serene waters dappled with moonlight. It might not have had an impressive mountain range in the background like the one back home did, but the creek was stunning in its own way.

Dustin cut the engine and opened the driver's side door. "This is how we do it down South," he said.

I opened my own door and followed him out to the creek, about to ask why we were here. Before I got the chance, he kicked off his shoes and cast his shirt on a low branch hanging over the creek. Without another word, he dove headfirst into the water. The water rippled out around him as he swam through the creek. I couldn't help but smile as I watched his face illuminated in the moonlight. He was clearly in his element, riding the Georgia waters with the ease of someone who'd been living here his whole life.

His head broke through the smooth surface of the water, and he smiled at me. "Come on in. The water's fine."

I looked down at my tank top, which had been sticking to my body in the heat during the drive here. A dip in the water sounded tempting. But my reservations made me pause just before the mouth of the creek.

"Are you sure that water is clean?"

"Come on, Bailey. Don't overthink it. Just let yourself feel for once."

I took two wary steps toward the creek, where there was a flash of movement in the grass. It looked like a clump of dirt at first. A large, hairy clump of dirt that happened to have eight legs. Up until then, I'd never seen a live tarantula—and definitely not one that was crawling mere inches away from my bare leg.

I shrieked and stumbled forward, only for my foot to land in the mud-laden lining of the creek. I slid and lost my balance before falling straight into the creek. The salty water engulfed me, making my eyes burn. After a moment, I came up for air, gasping. I squeezed the excess water out of my hair and wiped my eyes, trying to refocus my vision.

I looked up to see Dustin doubled over with laughter. Once

he caught his breath, he said, "Looks like the creek chose for ya."

I splashed him in response, which only made him laugh again. I planted my hands on my hips. "Well, since I'm already in here, I bet you can't beat me to the end of the creek."

He stopped laughing and put his game face on. "Oh, you're on."

I couldn't have been more grateful that I had a cousin who swam competitively. She'd given me pointers that I put to good use now as I flew past Dustin. When my hand touched the muddy bank on the opposite end of the creek, I held up a fist in victory. Dustin lagged behind me, taking labored breaths. I pretended to look at an imaginary stopwatch as I waited for him to catch up to me.

When he finally reached the finish line, he took a moment to catch his breath. "Where in the hell did you learn to swim that fast?"

"It's a secret," I said with a grin.

He wrapped his arms around my waist. "I thought you said no more secrets between us."

I gently pressed my lips to his chest. "I did." I tilted my face up toward his, my breath tickling his beard. "I'm an open book, if you're ready to read it."

His brown eyes darkened with desire, and he pulled me to him, his fingers grasping my hair. In the milky glow of the moonlight, he kissed me long and deep. As I lost myself in the moment, I thought back to what he'd told me earlier: *Don't overthink it. Just let yourself feel for once.* Standing there in the middle of the creek with his body against mine, I let all my thoughts go and allowed my feelings to take the wheel. And it made the moment that much more beautiful.

When we pulled apart, a lazy smile spread across his face. "Well, that makes up for losing to you just now."

I laughed. "You're gonna have to take lessons to catch up to me next time."

A cool breeze passed over me then, and I wrapped my arms around myself. Dustin reached over and touched my arm. "Are you cold? I got towels in the truck if you're ready to dry off."

I nodded. We stepped out of the creek, dripping wet on our way to the truck. He handed me a towel and grabbed one for himself. After drying off, we hopped up into the bed of his truck and lay side by side, gazing up at the peaceful night sky. I rested my head on his chest while he stroked my hair.

"Dustin?"

"Mm?"

"Why did you build that toy chest for Leah?"

He waved me off. "That ol' thing? It was nothin'. Just part of my job."

"But you didn't have to do it. You did it because you wanted to. And it made her so happy."

"Bailey, your family is my family. I've known Cassidy and your nieces almost as long as I've known you. If it makes her happy, it makes you happy. And that makes me one darn happy guy."

I stared up at the stars and said, "Do you remember the first day we saw each other again at the hardware store?"

"Course I do."

"You asked me if I was still afraid of being happy. And I was. But I'm not anymore. And it took me this long to understand it's because I trust you. I'm not saying there won't ever be disappointments, because there will be. But I know those obstacles won't be the end of the road for us. What we have here is real, and that doesn't just disappear. I can't tell you how many times I thought *this is too good to be true* in my life. And many times, it was. But this isn't. I feel… safe. The kind of safe you feel when you know something is yours to keep."

His eyes held the understanding I prayed they would. "There's always good mixed in with the bad. I was at my worst when I left for Georgia. And I'm still hurting. Will be for a long time. But all the fun we just had showed me that you can still smile while your heart is broken. You just need the right person to remind you of that from time to time."

I leaned in to kiss him again. When I pulled my lips away from his, I said, "And we can visit Mapleville whenever you want. I see how happy you are here. It's your home, after all."

He smiled. "I appreciate that. But Oak Plains is my real home. Wouldn't dream of being anywhere else."

Before I could get cozy with him again, Dustin's phone started ringing. He glanced at the display. "It's my dad."

I nodded, and he answered the call. "Hey, Dad." There was a long pause. I waited anxiously, wondering what his father had to tell him. He'd still been in Mapleville when Dustin and I drove in this morning. Dustin and his siblings had been taking care of him ever since Kelsea passed. Any parent would be shattered after a tragedy of that magnitude, but his dad had health concerns that needed to be closely monitored on top of everything else. For now, he seemed stable, but Dustin and I were constantly on edge.

"Okay. Sure. Yeah, I'll tell her."

Worry lingered on my face after he hung up. "Is everything all right?"

He nodded. "He said he wants to talk to you when we get home."

"Me?"

"That's what the old man said."

He must have seen the concern on my face, because he smiled warmly. "Don't sweat it, Bailey. He's real easy to talk to."

If he was anything like his son, I knew that would be true. As I followed Dustin into his truck, I tried to focus on how well things were going between us and held off on any concerns that were battling for my attention. Despite his reassurances, though, I could sense that Dustin was a bit on edge too. He didn't play any music on the ride home, his face closed and serious.

When we reached his childhood home, I hopped out of the cab and slowly made my way to the front door. Dustin opened it gingerly and stepped inside with me.

There was a hush permeating through the house that made it seem like no one was home. Dustin poked his head into several rooms before stopping in the living room. He exchanged a few words with his father and nodded at me. "I'll let you two chat," he said. On his way out, he squeezed my hand and gave me a meaningful smile. That simple gesture immediately melted the tension in my shoulders and helped me feel more at ease.

I rounded the corner to find Dustin's dad seated on the couch. I couldn't help but notice that the brown hair Dustin had inherited from him had gone almost entirely gray, and the deep lines on his face told the story of a parent who'd endured unthinkable grief. My heart sank as I looked at him. Slowly, I leaned in to give the older man a hug. "Good to see you, Mr. Cooper." I started to ask how he was, but the question died on my tongue. Of course he wasn't doing well. Who would be in his situation?

"You too, Bailey." He motioned for me to sit, so I lowered

myself onto the old leather couch across from him.

He didn't speak right away. At first, he looked down with his lips pressed together, as if he was about to tell me something painful. My heart fluttered with nerves as I waited.

Finally, his eyes met mine. "I understand you're romantically involved with my son?"

I nodded, my folded hands beginning to sweat in my lap. "Yes, sir."

He gave a short nod before pausing again. After a weighted silence, he said, "Dustin's got a huge heart. But he's been through hell and back. And I don't just mean with his family. He got his heart broken real bad in the past. A girl he really loved. Even though it was a long time ago, I can see how it affects him to this day."

He looked straight at me then. "I don't want to see my boy hurt again. I need to know that the girl he ends up with is going to treat him right and make him happy. We're all going through a lot right now, and I don't think he can deal with another heartbreak." His gaze grew deeper. "Can you promise me that?"

I rose from the couch and sat beside him, taking his leathery hands in mine. "I know exactly what it feels like to go through heartache. When Dustin left for Georgia, it felt like my whole world was coming apart. That was when I knew I couldn't stand the thought of living without him. We've both been hurt, and we both know how it can ruin a person. I know that what we have is different than anything I've had with anyone else.

"I'll tell you what I can't promise you. I can't promise you that everything will be smooth sailing. I can't promise you that we'll never have disagreements or get upset with each other. Those things will happen. And when they do, we'll just have to work harder to rise above them.

"What I can promise you is that I love your son. And I'll do everything I can to make sure he feels happy and loved."

He didn't respond for a beat, leaving me to anxiously run through my words in my head. But when he squeezed my hand and smiled, my heart swelled with relief.

"Thank you," he said, and I nodded, thinking he was talking about the promise I'd made. But then he looked into my eyes and added, "For coming into his life."

The room went blurry as a layer of mist covered my eyes. I swallowed. "I'm thankful too," I said quietly.

A tinge of something was slinking its way through me. A familiar echo of a feeling that used to be home to me. Before I went to see where Dustin was, I slipped into the guest room and dug through my suitcase, looking for the notebook I always carried with me now. I pulled it out and sat on the bed before opening to where I left off. On the page in front of me sat the first song I'd written after Dustin and I had gone swimming in the creek. Madison was right. Doing something worth singing about had made all the difference. A small smile snuck up on me as I read through the lyrics again, reliving the flurry of emotions I'd felt then.

I turned to a blank page and started scribbling down everything that was going on inside me. I needed to get it all down before it eluded me. As I wrote, I was surprised to find that I had more than just one song inside me. The words bled onto the next page, and the next, until I had nothing left to unpack.

I sat back and looked through the potential songs I'd just crafted. I didn't have my guitar with me, but I could already hear the melody that would carry every lyric. Just imagining giving life to each tune made me restless with excitement.

I stared out the window at the darkened countryside that

stretched out in front of me. Beholding its beauty, I felt a warmth fill me from deep within. This was what inspired me to make music. A peaceful night like this, a house full of people who loved and cared about me, and a contentment that reminded me of how lucky I was. It reminded me of what had drawn me to country music in the first place. And there was no better time than now to rekindle that flame.

I reached for my phone and tapped the Twitter icon. After hitting the new tweet button, I typed out the message I knew everyone who loved my music wanted to hear:

New music coming very shortly. And don't worry—it's the old Bailey again.

Chapter 20

The mid-October wind rustled Evelyn's tresses as she stared at me, dumbfounded. I was back home in Oak Plains, where my band was gearing up for my performance. "You're telling me it was hot enough to go swimming at the end of September?" Evelyn shook her head. "Even if I wasn't in love with Dustin, I'd be packing my bags and moving to Georgia right now."

"He swears he wouldn't want to be anywhere but here."

"That's only because you live here. Duh."

I nodded in the direction of the tall, dark-haired man standing near the refreshments table. "Why don't you ask Brett if he's interested in moving somewhere warmer?"

Evelyn's cheeks colored at the mention of her new boyfriend. "I already know the answer to that question. He'd move to Siberia before moving to a place where you need to have the AC on twenty-four, seven."

I smirked. "You finally find someone, and he hates the heat? You really know how to pick 'em."

"Don't rub it in," she said.

I laughed, undeterred by her sour mood. After sharing my new songs with Dustin in Georgia, I'd decided I wanted to perform them for everyone in Oak Plains. It only seemed right to let the people I loved hear my new music before I let the rest of the world hear it. After making some arrangements, Cassidy, Evelyn, and I had set up an outdoor concert at Alcott Park, the usual site of the annual summer concert. It was unseasonably warm for this time of year, which was perfect for an outdoor show. This time, though, I was the only one performing. I'd wanted it to be a scaled-down version of the summer event, with just my friends, family, and a smattering of Oak Plains residents there to cheer me on. Eventually, I would plan a bigger tour, but for now, I needed to get back to my roots. To remember where I came from.

"I'm glad you're happy," Evelyn said. She gave a wry smile. "And I bet your fans are, too, after that train wreck you released."

I punched her arm teasingly. "I was experimenting."

"With what? Emo music from the 2000s?"

"At least it got people's attention," I said defensively. At the look on her face, I rolled my eyes. "Okay, it was a disaster. But that'll just make my new music even better by comparison."

"If that's how you want to look at it."

My phone buzzed in my pocket, and I pulled it out to reveal Jackie's name flashing across the screen. "Hold on. I'll just be a minute."

I moved to a quieter spot toward the back of the park before answering. "Hello?"

"Bailey. Thank goodness you're alive. I know you're back in

the country for good, but please tell me you still care about the fate of your suburban house."

I smiled. "Of course I do. Any updates?"

Once I'd settled back in my hometown, I knew I needed to do something about my house in Ackerdale. I had no intention of living there again, which meant it was time to find a more suitable owner in the long term. Jackie, who was good friends with a local real estate agent, had taken it upon herself to ensure that my home found the right kind of person. I couldn't have been more grateful that she'd volunteered to take on the task—not only because I couldn't be in Ackerdale to oversee the process but because I could focus on my music back home now. And, of course, spend as much time with Dustin as possible.

"Oh, do I have *updates*. First of all, there are more people looking to move into suburban PA than I thought. I guess it doesn't hurt that we're so close to Pittsburgh. Speaking of which, we had a couple from Jersey swing by today, and I'm pretty sure the husband is dragging his wife here just so he can take her to as many Steelers games as he wants. The first thing he asked was how long it takes to get to Heinz Field from here. Dude rolled up in full Steelers gear and everything. Honestly, he would probably be in the city if he had his way. But I can tell he was trying to compromise." She paused. "Where was I going with this?"

I smiled to myself. A part of me missed my friend's penchant for going off on tangents. "Did you find any prospective homebuyers?" I prompted her.

"Oh, right! You won't believe this. A woman a little older than you stopped by, and we got to chatting. Turns out she's a singer too! Who would've thought? As soon as she said that, I knew she was the right person. I mean, what better legacy for your house? Imagine your home being filled with music and singing long after you leave."

"That sounds amazing, Jackie. Really. Thank you so much."

"No prob. Oh, and I'm so sorry I couldn't come to your concert. I'll be there in spirit. Make sure you send plenty of pictures."

"I will." I glanced up at the stage, where my band was just finishing setting up. "I have to go, actually. I'm on in a few minutes."

"Break a leg! Or whatever the equivalent of that is for concerts."

When I returned to the crowd, I saw Cassidy approaching with both kids in tow. She grinned the whole time. My sister had been doing a lot of grinning ever since I reunited with Dustin. I couldn't blame her. She was a sucker for happy endings.

"Where's your prince?" she asked.

I snorted. "He had to use the bathroom. And I'm pretty sure the line for the porta potties is longer than the food line."

She wrinkled her nose and scanned the scene around us. "Sure is quite the turnout. Even after all these years, everyone cancels their Saturday afternoon plans for a chance to hear you sing."

"What songs are you going to sing?" Leah asked, bouncing on her heels.

"It's a surprise."

"You should cover an Electric Ashes song," Jade said with a grin.

I laughed. "I doubt I could pull that off, but that would definitely be interesting." I smiled at my older niece. "How's school going? Make any new friends?" I asked, remembering that Jade had had a bumpy ride last year with her so-called friends ostracizing her.

Her face brightened. "You won't believe it, Aunt Bailey. A group of ninth graders let me sit with them at lunch yesterday. It's, like, an unspoken rule that the ninth graders don't even look at the eighth graders. But they let me hang out with them the whole time. Jenna looked *so* mad. It was the best."

I briefly considered telling her that her main goal shouldn't be to anger her enemies, but I decided to just let her be happy. "I'm so glad to hear that. Sounds like you're starting eighth grade on the right foot." I turned to Leah. "How's my little second grader doing?"

"Okay." She shrugged. "My teacher's always in a bad mood. I heard her tell another teacher that her husband can't 'get it up' anymore. Whatever that means."

It took every ounce of self-control inside me not to burst out laughing. Cassidy, whose face was red with restraint, jerked her head to the right. "Speaking of getting it up…"

I turned and saw Dustin coming our way. As he pulled me into his arms, I buried my face in his neck, luxuriating in the smell of him. "I was worried you got lost or something. You know I can't get up on stage without a good-luck kiss."

"Gross," Jade muttered.

Dustin chuckled as we pulled away from each other. "I guess she doesn't want to see the old people make out, huh?"

Cassidy smirked. "If you're planning on making out with her, please move away from my children."

"Don't worry," I said, my gaze still fixed on Dustin's face. "We'll save it for after the show."

"I'll be cheering you on right here," he said.

His words flung me all the way back to the summer concert,

and my stomach dipped with dread. He *had* been there to cheer me on—or at least I'd thought he had been. Until I returned backstage to find no sign of him. And everyone knew how that story had ended.

Cassidy must have sensed my sudden change in demeanor, because she gently touched my arm. "It's not like that anymore," she said softly, reading my mind in the way only sisters could. "This is your chance to start fresh. Break the spell."

Break the spell. I knew she was referring to Dustin's disappearance at the last show and the fire at the show before that. I hadn't noticed until now that I was bracing myself for something bad to happen after today's concert. That was the pattern I'd come to learn. But maybe she was right. Maybe this was my chance to break the spell I'd fallen into and have a fully enjoyable concert—from beginning to end.

I gave her an appreciative smile before making my way to the stage. The chairs dotting the lawn were nearly filled now, creating a mass of eager fans whose eyes were fixed to the stage I was about to step onto. It was only a tiny fraction of the audience that had gathered at the Apex Center in August, but it still reminded me of that concert. A bundle of nerves gathered in my stomach, making my legs feel unsteady as I headed toward the steps.

I was just about to climb the steps when I glimpsed someone standing by them. "Madison?" I walked over and hugged her. "I'm so glad you came."

"Of course. I wouldn't miss it." She squeezed my hand. "Good luck. Not that you need it anyway."

I looked out over the crowd again and felt another wave of nerves wash over me. In spite of myself, I forced a smile. "Thanks. I'll see you after the show."

Chapter 20

I stepped onto the small, makeshift stage where Evelyn was already standing with her guitar. She smiled when she saw me. "Here we are again."

"It's my first time on this stage since that last show six years ago," I said, hoping she didn't pick up on the trepidation in my voice.

She studied me closely. "You're not nervous, are you?"

"Just a little," I said, shrugging. "But that's to be expected."

Before she could say anything more, I strode up to the microphone at the front of the stage. I tested it and peered out at the audience that now had its attention on me. "Thanks for coming out, everyone."

Applause and cheers broke out as I smiled. "The summer concert this year was held in Pittsburgh, as I'm sure most of you know. Even though it was a lot of fun to perform in such a big venue, I'm happy to be back where it all started." I looked down at the guitar strapped across my chest. "I wrote some new songs for y'all, and I can't wait for you to hear them. I wanted to make sure everyone in my hometown got an exclusive preview before I officially release new music." I turned to my best friend. "Take it away, Ev."

She started to play, and I let the tune carry me as I jumped into the lyrics. I was having way too much fun for my nerves to stick around. The music buoyed me like it always did, lifting me up and away from the outside world. For now, I didn't have to be anyone but Bailey Flynn, the singer everyone had congregated here to see.

Halfway through the second song, I spotted Miranda and Wes standing toward the back of the crowd. Their baby carriage was parked next to them, a tiny bundle of joy strapped inside. My throat grew tight as I looked at them, but it wasn't out of jealousy or sadness. For the first time, I felt genuinely happy that another family was going to enjoy the same land that I'd been proud to call my home all those years ago. I smiled and waved at them, and they warmly returned the gesture. Letting go of the hurt made me feel freer than I had in a long time.

Toward the end of my set, I decided I wanted to have a little fun. After all, I'd arranged this concert out of a desire to celebrate. I walked over to Evelyn and whispered, "Let's do the Shania cover."

She looked at me dubiously. "But we haven't rehearsed it."

"We both know it by heart. Come on, let's have a little fun."

Evelyn still looked unsure until she faced the crowd. I didn't even have to follow her line of vision to know she was looking right at Dustin. As she turned back to me, her lips curved into an impish smile. "Oh, we have the *perfect* audience for that song."

I grinned and strode back up to the mic. "Y'all ready for something a little different?"

A resounding cheer answered that question. Evelyn began plucking the opening notes while nostalgia swept over me. My friend had learned "Any Man of Mine" on the guitar when she was only twelve, the same age I'd been when I learned the vocals. It was our favorite Shania Twain song, and we'd hardly done it justice all those years ago. But we'd both had ample time to practice and what resulted was a much more respectable version of the song. Besides, we both were having way too much fun to care how good we sounded.

I proudly belted out the lyrics that painted a picture of Shania's ideal man. And, really, any woman's ideal man. Dustin had moved closer to the stage somewhere between my second and third song, and he was sporting an amused smile as he watched me. I could tell he'd already figured out what I was doing. Seeing him loaded me up with a fresh supply of confidence, and I moved closer to the mic. "Come on up here, baby," I crooned.

He scaled the steps without hesitation and joined Evelyn and me onstage. With my arm draped around him, I said, "Ladies, I think we've all been with men who didn't fit this song. But when you find the one who does, it'll be well worth the wait."

Evelyn stopped playing and searched the crowd for a moment. She pointed at someone and said, "Brett, I know you feel a lot of pressure on you right now." She smiled sweetly. "And that's because there is."

Laughter rippled through the crowd, and I looked up at Dustin with a smile. "Don't worry. You already passed with flying colors."

He kissed the top of my head and held me through the rest of the song. When the last note dissolved into the air, our fans collectively got to their feet and cheered rambunctiously. I soaked up the sight of my hometown sharing my joy and passion for the music I made. Moments like this didn't come along often, and this was my chance to absorb every last drop before it was stored in my mind as a memory.

Once I was back on the lawn, Cassidy ambushed me with a hug. "That was *incredible*. You were having so much fun, and it showed."

I smiled. "I really was. I'm pretty sure that's true for everyone."

"I know I was," a familiar voice said. I turned around to see Madison standing behind me. "That reminded me of all the summer concerts I used to go to in the past. You really went back to your roots."

"I'm so glad I did." I faced my sister and Madison. "What did you think of the new music?"

"It was so you. And exactly the type of smash hit that would drive Lauren crazy, which makes it even better," Madison said.

"You already know what I think," Cassidy chimed in. "It's the type of music you were meant to make all along." Her eyes drifted behind my head. "What does the boyfriend think?"

I felt Dustin's arms around me before I saw him. "I think every second of it was perfect."

"Couldn't have guessed that," Evelyn muttered.

Madison turned to the refreshments table. "Anyone want to get something to eat? I think they still have some of the muffins left."

"Say no more," Cassidy said, heading straight to the table.

Evelyn and Madison followed, leaving just Dustin and me. He leaned down to kiss me. "Well, I'd say that was a successful concert."

"I'd say so too." I smiled as I looked around me. "And the best part is that no disaster happened at any point during the show."

Brushing a stray hair away from my eye, he said, "You didn't actually expect something to happen, did you?"

I shrugged. "I don't know. When you get burned twice, I guess you're always going to be on edge the third time."

He tilted my face up so I was looking directly at him. "I would never let you fall, Bailey. Ever. Please understand that."

His eyes were filled with love and sincerity, and I latched on with my entire being. "I know," I whispered.

I rested my head on his shoulder for a peaceful moment while an old Reba hit drifted out of the speakers. The smells of various foods wafted out from the refreshments table, tickling my nose. He turned toward the small crowd that had gathered there. "We could grab some food if you're hungry."

Chapter 20

A smile tugged at the corners of my mouth. "The concert isn't over yet, you know."

"What do you mean?"

I brushed my fingers down his chest. "I saved one last song just for you. If we get away from the crowds, I'll play it for you."

He studied me for a moment, as if weighing my offer. Then, without warning, he scooped me up in his arms. "You don't need to say another word, Bailey Flynn."

I laughed while he carried me all the way back to his truck. Cassidy was right. The spell had been broken—and in the best way possible.

The last few notes of the Reba song drifted on the wind, and I let the melody caress my ears. I no longer needed to brace myself for what would happen after the music. Because, in truth, it had never really stopped.

Acknowledgments

No book comes to fruition on its own, so I am indebted to many people for helping me bring this novel to life. As always, my heartfelt gratitude goes out to my mom and dad, who will always be my biggest fans and supporters of my art. To my mom, who is the most thorough beta reader any author could ask for, thank you for taking your time with going through my draft and giving honest feedback (even when I didn't always want to hear it). And to my sister, Christina—in the incredibly off-chance that my book gets made into a movie, I'll make sure they cast you to play the part of every character.

Thank you to my editor, Darlene, who challenged me to strengthen every aspect of my book from plot to character development. A good editor bridges the gap between what an author wrote and what they truly wanted to say. I appreciate you doing exactly that so I could tell my story in the best way possible.

To the wonderful writing community on social media, I'm

grateful to be a part of such an encouraging and supportive group of writers. I've met some amazing people who understand the struggles and triumphs of being an indie author. Thank you to everyone who has helped promote my book and supported my passion.

Last but not least, thank you to each and every one of my readers. It means the world to me that you're holding my book in your hands right now. I hope it brings you as much joy as it brought me while writing it and that you leave its pages better than you were before.

About the Author

Elena Goudelias is a contemporary romance and women's fiction author with a Bachelor of Arts in literature from Fordham University. A New Jersey native, Elena loves creating heartwarming stories full of vivid descriptions and lovable, lifelike characters. When she isn't writing, Elena enjoys reading voraciously, listening to country music, working out, and shopping. You can find Elena's work at elenagoudelias.com.

Also by Elena Goudelias

Beyond the Horizon

After losing out on a once-in-a-lifetime opportunity to join the New York fashion scene, Nora Evans left home and its disappointments behind without a second glance. Her new life, a peaceful existence on an Iowa dairy farm with her husband and two children, is worlds away from everything she's ever known. But when an old high school friend turns up in her one-horse town after fifteen years, she presents Nora with a second chance to live out the dream she left behind.

With the past at her heels, Nora must grapple with a haunting question: is the life she built for herself a model of personal success, or is it nothing more than a cover-up for the life she was truly meant to live?

CPSIA information can be obtained
at www.ICGtesting.com
Printed in the USA
BVHW091013120223
658366BV00027B/505

9 781088 103272